CONTENTS

beef 3

    cocoa-spiced beef tenderloin with pineapple salsa 5
    greek-style flank steak with tangy yogurt sauce 6
    stir-fried orange beef 7
    mediterranean kabobs 9
    beef steak with carrots and mint 10
    broiled sirloin with spicy mustard and apple chutney 11
    beef steak with light tomato mushroom sauce 12
    japanese-style beef and noodle soup 14
    quick beef casserole 16

poultry 17

    moroccan chicken stew with couscous 18
    thai-style chicken curry 20
    sweet-and-sour chicken 22
    chicken quesadillas with red and green salsa 23
    chicken and mushroom fricassee 25
    chicken and celery stir-fry 26
    oven-crusted chicken breast 27
    chicken picadillo 28
    chicken ratatouille 29
    asian-style chicken wraps 30
    cornbread-crusted turkey 32
    turkey club burger 35

turkey mole 36
20-minute chicken creole 38

seafood 39

grilled tuna with chickpea and spinach salad 41
baja-style salmon tacos 42
spanish-style shrimp stew 43
braised cod with leeks 45
baked red snapper with zesty tomato sauce 47
teriyaki-glazed salmon with stir-fried vegetables 48
red snapper provencal 49
asian-style steamed salmon 51
baked salmon dijon 52
fish veronique 53

pork 55

pork mignons with french applesauce 57
pork chops in warm cherry sauce 58
baked pork chops 59
grilled pork tenderloin with asian sauce 61

main-dish pastas 63

cold fusilli pasta with summer vegetables 65
mushroom penne 66
rotini with spicy red pepper and almond sauce 67
pasta caprese 69
linguini with clam sauce 70
heavenly chicken with angel hair pasta 71
whole-wheat bow tie pasta with puttanesca sauce 73
turkey bolognese with shell pasta 74
lemon and garlic pasta with pan-seared scallops 76
classic macaroni and cheese 78
sweet and sour seashells 79

vegetarian main-dish meals 81

- tuscan beans with tomatoes and oregano 83
- caribbean casserole 84
- red beans and rice 85
- corn and black bean burritos 87
- lentils with brown rice and kale 88
- broccoli with asian tofu 90
- three-bean chili with chunky tomatoes 92
- caribbean pink beans 93
- edamame stew 95
- tofu stir-fry with spicy sauce 96

side dishes 99

vegetable side dishes 101

- asparagus with lemon sauce 103
- cauliflower with whole-wheat breadcrumbs 104
- grilled romaine lettuce with caesar dressing 105
- baby spinach with golden raisins and pine nuts 107
- roasted beets with orange sauce 109
- autumn salad 110
- limas and spinach 111
- cinnamon-glazed baby carrots 113
- creamy squash soup with shredded apples 114

grain side dishes 115

- couscous with carrots, walnuts, and raisins 117
- quinoa with paprika and cumin 118
- good-for-you cornbread 119
- savory brown rice 121
- kasha with bell pepper confetti 122
- parmesan rice and pasta pilaf 123
- pesto baked polenta 125
- sunshine rice 126

cocoa-spiced beef tenderloin with pineapple salsa

Latin American flavors come alive in this festive beef dish with fruity salsa

Prep time: 20 minutes
Cook time: 20 minutes

½ Tbsp	vegetable oil
1	beef tenderloin roast (16 oz)

For salsa:

½ C	canned diced pineapple, in fruit juice, chopped into small pieces
¼ C	red onion, minced
2 tsp	fresh cilantro, rinsed, dried, and chopped (or substitute ¼ tsp dried coriander)
1 Tbsp	lemon juice

For seasoning:

1 tsp	ground black pepper
1 tsp	ground coriander
1 Tbsp	ground cinnamon
¼ tsp	ground allspice
1 Tbsp	cocoa powder (unsweetened)
2 tsp	chili powder
¼ tsp	salt

1. Preheat oven to 375 °F.
2. For the salsa, combine all ingredients and toss well. Let sit for 10–15 minutes to marinate while preparing the seasoning and cooking the meat.
3. For the beef tenderloin seasoning, combine all ingredients. Lightly oil the tenderloin and spread an even layer of the dry seasoning over the entire roast.
4. Place the seasoned roast on a roasting or broiling pan and roast for 10–15 minutes (to a minimum internal temperature of 145 °F). Let cool for 5 minutes before carving into 16 slices (1 ounce each).
5. Serve four slices of the tenderloin with ¼ cup salsa on the side.

Tip: Delicious with a side of rice and **Grilled Romaine Lettuce With Caesar Dressing** (on page 105).

yield: 4 servings

serving size: 4 oz tenderloin roast, ¼ C salsa

each serving provides:

calories	215	total fiber	2 g
total fat	9 g	protein	25 g
saturated fat	3 g	carbohydrates	9 g
cholesterol	67 mg	potassium	451 mg
sodium	226 mg		

deliciously healthy dinners

greek-style flank steak with tangy yogurt sauce

Prep time: 25 minutes
Cook time: 25 minutes

lemon, garlic, and oregano bring out the flavors of this bold and flavorful Mediterranean dish

1	beef flank steak (12 oz)

For marinade:

¼ C	lemon juice
1 Tbsp	olive oil
2 tsp	fresh oregano, rinsed, dried, and chopped (or ½ tsp dried)
1 Tbsp	garlic, minced (about 2–3 cloves)

For yogurt sauce:

1 C	cucumber, peeled, seeded, and chopped
1 C	nonfat plain yogurt
2 Tbsp	lemon juice
1 Tbsp	fresh dill, rinsed, dried, and chopped (or 1 tsp dried)
1 Tbsp	garlic, minced (about 2–3 cloves)
½ tsp	salt

1. For the marinade, combine lemon juice, olive oil, oregano, and garlic in a large bowl.
2. Lay steak in a flat container with sides and pour marinade over the steak. Let the steak marinate for at least 20 minutes or up to 24 hours, turning several times.
3. Combine all the ingredients for the yogurt sauce. Set yogurt sauce aside for at least 15 minutes to blend flavors. (Sauce can be prepared up to 1 hour in advance and refrigerated.)
4. Preheat oven broiler on high temperature, with the rack 3 inches from heat source.
5. Broil steak for about 10 minutes on each side (to a minimum internal temperature of 145 °F). Let cool for 5 minutes before carving.
6. Slice thinly across the grain into 12 slices (1 ounce each).*
7. Serve three slices of the steak with ½ cup yogurt sauce on the side.

Tip: Try serving in a sandwich with pita bread, lettuce, and tomato.

* For description of how to cut meat across the grain, see FAQs in appendix C (on page 135).

yield: 4 servings

serving size: 3 oz steak, ½ C yogurt sauce

each serving provides:

calories	181	total fiber	less than 1 g
total fat	7 g	protein	21 g
saturated fat	2 g	carbohydrates	9 g
cholesterol	36 mg	potassium	329 mg
sodium	364 mg		

stir-fried orange beef

Prep time: 10 minutes
Cook time: 20 minutes

tangy orange-flavored beef with crisp vegetables

1 bag	(12 oz) frozen vegetable stir-fry
1 Tbsp	peanut or vegetable oil
1 Tbsp	onion, minced (or ½ Tbsp dried)
1 Tbsp	garlic, minced (about 2–3 cloves)
1 Tbsp	ginger, minced
1	egg white, lightly beaten (or *substitute liquid egg white*)
2 Tbsp	cornstarch
12 oz	beef flank steak, sliced into thin strips
3 Tbsp	Hoisin sauce
1 Tbsp	lite soy sauce
½ C	orange juice
1 Tbsp	dry sherry (optional)

1. Thaw frozen vegetables in the microwave (or place entire bag in a bowl of hot water for about 10 minutes). Set aside until step 7.
2. Heat oil in a large wok or sauté pan.
3. Add onion, garlic, and ginger and stir fry until tender but not brown, about 30 seconds to 1 minute.
4. Put egg white in one bowl and cornstarch in another. Dip steak strips into egg white and then coat with cornstarch.
5. Add steak strips to pan and continue to stir fry until steak strips are lightly browned, about 5–8 minutes.
6. Add Hoisin sauce, soy sauce, orange juice, and sherry (optional), and bring to a boil over high heat. Immediately lower temperature to a gentle simmer.
7. Add the thawed vegetables and mix gently. Simmer until vegetables are heated through, about 3–4 minutes.
8. Divide mixture into four equal portions (about 2 cups each) and serve.

Tip: Delicious over rice or Asian-style noodles (soba or udon).

yield:
4 servings

serving size:
2 C meat and vegetables

each serving provides:

calories	261	total fiber	3 g
total fat	9 g	protein	23 g
saturated fat	2 g	carbohydrates	23 g
cholesterol	28 mg	potassium	648 mg
sodium	418 mg		

deliciously healthy dinners

mediterranean kabobs

Prep time: 15 minutes
Cook time: 10 minutes

broiled beef and chicken cubes flavored with lemon and parsley

For marinade:

2 Tbsp	olive oil
1 Tbsp	garlic, minced (about 2–3 cloves)
2 Tbsp	lemon juice
1 Tbsp	fresh parsley, rinsed, dried, and chopped (or 1 tsp dried)
½ tsp	salt

For kabobs:

6 oz	top sirloin or other beef steak cubes (12 cubes)
6 oz	boneless, skinless chicken breast, cut into ¾-inch cubes (12 cubes)
1	large white onion, cut into ¾-inch squares (12 pieces)
12	cherry tomatoes, rinsed
1	(4 oz) red bell pepper, rinsed and cut into ¾-inch squares (12 squares)
12	wooden or metal skewers, each 6 inches long (if wood, soak them in warm water for 5–10 minutes to prevent burning)

1. Preheat grill pan or oven broiler (with the rack 3 inches from heat source) on high temperature.
2. Combine ingredients for marinade, and divide between two bowls (one bowl to marinate the raw meat and one bowl for cooking and serving).
3. Mix the beef, chicken, onion, tomatoes, and red pepper cubes in one bowl of the marinade and let sit. After 5 minutes, discard remaining marinade.
4. Place one piece of beef, chicken, tomato, onion, and red pepper on each of the 12 skewers.
5. Grill or broil on each of the four sides for 2–3 minutes or until completely cooked (to a minimum internal temperature of 145 °F for beef and 165 °F for chicken). Spoon most of the second half of the marinade over the kebabs while cooking.
6. Serve three skewers per serving. Drizzle the remaining marinade on top of each kebab before serving (use only the marinade that did not touch the raw meat or chicken).

Tip: Delicious served over orzo pasta or rice with a side of **Asparagus With Lemon Sauce** (on page 103).

yield: 4 servings
serving size: 3 skewers

each serving provides:

calories	202	total fiber	2 g
total fat	11 g	protein	18 g
saturated fat	2 g	carbohydrates	9 g
cholesterol	40 mg	potassium	431 mg
sodium	333 mg		

deliciously healthy dinners

beef steak with carrots and mint

Prep time: 15 minutes
Cook time: 15 minutes

a winning combination—a cool, crisp salad with a hot, juicy steak

For steak:

4	beef top sirloin steaks, lean (3 oz each)
¼ tsp	salt
¼ tsp	ground black pepper
½ Tbsp	olive oil

For salad:

1 C	carrots, rinsed and grated
1 C	cucumber, rinsed, peeled, and sliced
1 Tbsp	olive oil
2 Tbsp	fresh mint, rinsed, dried, and shredded (or ½ Tbsp dried)
¼ tsp	salt
¼ tsp	ground black pepper
½ C	orange juice

1. For the steaks, preheat grill pan or oven broiler (with the rack 3 inches from heat source) on high temperature.

2. For the salad, combine all the ingredients in a bowl, and mix gently. Marinate salad for at least 5–10 minutes to blend flavors before serving. (Salad can be made up to 3 hours in advance and refrigerated.)

3. Season the steaks with salt and pepper, and lightly coat with oil.

4. Grill or broil 2–3 minutes on each side, or to your desired doneness (to a minimum internal temperature of 145 °F).

5. Remove from the heat and let cool for 5 minutes.

6. Serve one 3-ounce steak with ½ cup salad on the side.

Tip: Try serving with **Couscous With Carrots, Walnuts, and Raisins** (on page 117).

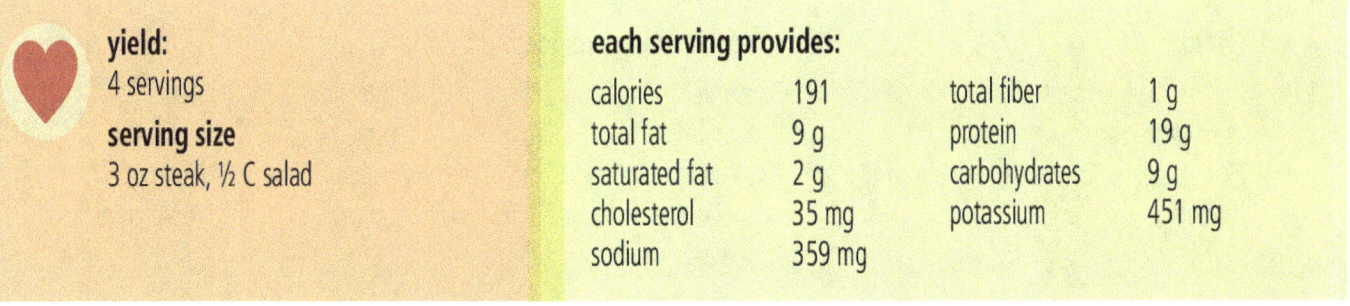

yield:
4 servings

serving size
3 oz steak, ½ C salad

each serving provides:

calories	191	total fiber	1 g
total fat	9 g	protein	19 g
saturated fat	2 g	carbohydrates	9 g
cholesterol	35 mg	potassium	451 mg
sodium	359 mg		

broiled sirloin with spicy mustard and apple chutney

Prep time: 15 minutes
Cook time: 30 minutes

spicy mustard dressing and sweet-and-sour apple chutney make a tangy combination to excite your taste buds

For chutney:

1	Granny Smith apple, rinsed, peeled, cored, and diced (about 1 C)
2 Tbsp	shallots, minced
1 Tbsp	garlic, minced (about 2–3 cloves)
½ C	canned no-salt-added diced tomatoes
2 oz	golden seedless raisins (about ½ C)
¼ C	apple cider vinegar
2 Tbsp	maple syrup

For steak:

4	beef top sirloin steaks, lean (3 oz each)
¼ tsp	salt
¼ tsp	ground black pepper
1 Tbsp	olive oil

For mustard dressing:

2 C	low-sodium beef broth
2 Tbsp	Dijon mustard
2 Tbsp	cornstarch

1. For the chutney, combine all the ingredients in a small saucepan. Bring to a boil over high heat, and simmer for 20 minutes or until apples are cooked and soft. Remove from the heat and hold warm, or cool and store.

2. For the steaks, preheat grill pan or oven broiler (with the rack 3 inches from heat source) on high temperature.

3. Season the steaks with salt and pepper, and lightly coat with oil.

4. Grill or broil 3–4 minutes on each side, or to your desired doneness (to a minimum internal temperature of 145 °F). Remove from the heat and set aside for 5 minutes.

5. For the mustard dressing, mix together beef broth, Dijon mustard, and cornstarch in a small saucepan. Bring to a boil on medium-high heat while stirring constantly. Lower the heat, and simmer for 2–3 minutes.

6. Serve each steak with ¼ cup of chutney and ½ cup of mustard dressing.

Tip: Try serving with a side of steamed broccoli and **Savory Brown Rice** (on page 121).

yield: 4 servings

serving size: 3 oz steak, ¼ C chutney, ½ C mustard dressing

each serving provides:

calories	285	total fiber	2 g
total fat	8 g	protein	23 g
saturated fat	2 g	carbohydrates	32 g
cholesterol	35 mg	potassium	554 mg
sodium	421 mg		

beef steak with light tomato mushroom sauce

Prep time: 10 minutes
Cook time: 25 minutes

try serving with crusty bread to soak up the incredibly flavorful sauce

1 Tbsp	olive oil
4	beef top sirloin steaks, lean (3 oz each)
4 oz	white mushrooms, rinsed and quartered (about 1 C)
1	large shallot, minced (about 2 Tbsp)
1 Tbsp	garlic, minced (about 2–3 cloves)
1 C	canned no-salt-added diced tomatoes
2 Tbsp	no-salt-added tomato paste
2 Tbsp	apple cider vinegar
2 C	low-sodium beef broth
1 Tbsp	cornstarch
1 Tbsp	fresh parsley, rinsed, dried, and minced (or 1 tsp dried)
1 Tbsp	fresh tarragon, rinsed, dried, and chopped (or 1 tsp dried)
½ tsp	salt
¼ tsp	ground black pepper

1. Preheat oven to 350 °F.
2. Heat olive oil in a large, heavy-bottom sauté pan.
3. Gently blot steaks dry with paper towels and then carefully place them in the hot pan.
4. Sauté both sides, about 2–3 minutes, until golden to dark brown.
5. Remove steaks from pan, and put them on a baking sheet to finish in the preheated oven for an additional 3–5 minutes or to your desired doneness (to a minimum internal temperature of 145 °F).
6. To make the sauce, pour off any excess grease from the pan. Add mushrooms and sauté until lightly brown, about 3–4 minutes.
7. Lower the heat, and add shallot and garlic. Cook gently over low heat for about 2 minutes, until tender, but not brown.
8. Add tomatoes, tomato paste, and apple cider vinegar, and cook an additional 3 minutes.
9. In a bowl, mix beef broth and cornstarch.

continued on page 13

beef steak with light tomato mushroom sauce (continued)

10. Add broth mixture, parsley, and tarragon to the sauté pan. Bring to a boil on medium-high heat while stirring constantly. Lower the heat and simmer for 2–3 minutes. Season with salt and pepper.

11. Serve one steak with ½ cup sauce.

Tip: Also pairs nicely with **Cauliflower With Whole-Wheat Breadcrumbs** (on page 104).

yield: 4 servings

serving size: 3 oz steak, ½ C sauce

each serving provides:

calories	200	total fiber	2 g
total fat	8 g	protein	23 g
saturated fat	2 g	carbohydrates	10 g
cholesterol	35 mg	potassium	569 mg
sodium	404 mg		

japanese-style beef and noodle soup

Prep time: 25 minutes
Cook time: 15 minutes

this hearty main-meal soup is flavorful, yet simple to prepare

For broth:

4 oz	shiitake mushroom stems, rinsed (remove caps and set aside) *(or substitute dried shiitake mushrooms)*
1 Tbsp	garlic, minced (about 2–3 cloves)
1 Tbsp	ginger, minced
1 stalk	lemongrass, crushed *(or the zest from 1 lemon: Use a peeler to grate a thin layer of skin off a lemon)*
1 Tbsp	ground coriander
4 C	low-sodium beef broth
1 Tbsp	lite soy sauce

For meat and vegetables:

1 bag	(12 oz) frozen vegetable stir-fry
4 oz	shiitake mushrooms caps, rinsed and quartered
8 oz	udon or soba noodles *(or substitute angel hair pasta)*, cooked
1 lb	lean beef top sirloin, sliced very thin
4 oz	firm silken tofu, diced
¼ C	scallions (green onions), rinsed and sliced thin

1. Thaw frozen vegetables in the microwave (or place entire bag in a bowl of hot water for about 10 minutes). Set aside until step 4.

2. Combine all ingredients for broth, except soy sauce, in a medium-sized pot or saucepan. Bring to a boil over high heat, then lower heat and simmer for 15 minutes.

3. Strain the broth through a fine wire colander, and discard the solid parts. Season to taste with soy sauce.

continued on page 15

japanese-style beef and noodle soup (continued)

4. To finish the soup, bring the broth back to a boil. Add the thawed vegetable stir-fry mix and mushroom caps, and simmer for 1 minute.

5. Add the noodles and continue to simmer for another minute.

6. Add the beef and continue to simmer for about 5 minutes or until the beef is slightly pink to brown (to a minimum internal temperature of 145 °F).

7. Add tofu and scallions, and simmer 1–2 minutes until heated through.

8. Serve immediately in 1-cup portions.

Hint: There are several varieties of tofu, each with a different moisture level. Silken and soft tofu are the moistest and easily blended into shakes, dips, and dressings. Regular tofu is less moist, and it's best for scrambling or using like cheese in casseroles. Firm, extra-firm, and pressed tofu are the driest. They absorb other flavors easily and hold their shape in stir-fries and on the grill.

yield: 4 servings

serving size: 1 C soup

each serving provides:

calories	325	total fiber	4 g
total fat	8 g	protein	36 g
saturated fat	3 g	carbohydrates	28 g
cholesterol	52 mg	potassium	882 mg
sodium	285 mg		

quick beef casserole

Prep time: 10 minutes
Cook time: 45 minutes

lean beef, vegetables, and rice are tossed together in this quick and easy casserole

½ lb	lean ground beef
1 C	onion, chopped
1 C	celery, rinsed and chopped
1 C	green bell pepper, rinsed, seeded, and cubed
3½ C	tomatoes, rinsed and diced
¼ tsp	salt
½ tsp	ground black pepper
¼ tsp	paprika
1 C	frozen peas
2	small carrots, rinsed, peeled, and diced
1 C	uncooked rice
1½ C	water

1. In a sauté pan, brown the ground beef.
2. Drain off the extra fat by tilting the sauté pan over a disposable cup in the sink to collect the fat. Use the lid to shield the meat from falling out. After the fat has turned solid, discard the cup in the trash.
3. Add the rest of the ingredients to the sauté pan, and mix well.
4. Cover sauté pan with lid, and cook over medium heat until boiling.
5. Reduce to low heat and simmer for 35 minutes. Serve hot.

Tip: To save time, use no-salt-added canned tomatoes and frozen chopped peppers and carrots.

yield:
8 servings

serving size:
1½ C casserole

each serving provides:

calories	201	total fiber	3 g
total fat	5 g	protein	9 g
saturated fat	2 g	carbohydrates	31 g
cholesterol	16 mg	potassium	449 mg
sodium	164 mg		

moroccan chicken stew with couscous

Prep time: 15 minutes
Cook time: 30 minutes

spice it up with this traditional dish from northern Africa

1 Tbsp	olive oil
1 lb	skinless chicken legs, split (about 4 whole legs)
1 Tbsp	Moroccan spice blend*
1 C	carrots, rinsed, peeled, and diced
1 C	onion, diced
¼ C	lemon juice
2 C	low-sodium chicken broth
½ C	ripe black olives, sliced
¼ tsp	salt
1 Tbsp	chili sauce (optional)

For couscous:

1 C	low-sodium chicken broth
1 C	couscous *(try whole-wheat couscous)*
1 Tbsp	fresh mint, rinsed, dried, and shredded thin (or 1 tsp dried)

1. Heat olive oil in a large sauté pan. Add chicken legs, and brown on all sides, about 2–3 minutes per side. Remove chicken from pan and put on a plate with a cover to hold warm.

2. Add spice blend to sauté pan and toast gently.

3. Add carrots and onion to sauté pan, and cook for about 3–4 minutes or until the onions have turned clear, but not brown.

4. Add lemon juice, chicken broth, and olives to sauté pan, and bring to a boil over high heat. Add chicken legs, and return to a boil. Cover and gently simmer for about 10–15 minutes (to a minimum internal temperature of 165 °F).

continued on page 19

moroccan chicken stew with couscous (continued)

5. Meanwhile, prepare the couscous by bringing chicken broth to a boil in a saucepan. Add couscous, and remove from the heat. Cover and let stand for 10 minutes.

6. Fluff couscous with a fork, and gently mix in the mint.

7. When chicken is cooked, add salt. Serve two chicken legs over ½ cup couscous topped with ½ cup sauce in a serving bowl. Add chili sauce to taste.

main dishes

poultry

Tip: Try serving with a side of **Cinnamon-Glazed Baby Carrots** (on page 113).

* You also can make your own Moroccan spice blend by mixing 1 teaspoon each of ground coriander, ground cumin, ground ginger, and ground cinnamon per 1 pound of meat or chicken. Make this mix in advance and store it in your pantry to use as needed.

yield:
4 servings

serving size:
2 chicken legs, ½ C couscous, ½ C sauce

each serving provides:

calories	333	total fiber	6 g
total fat	12 g	protein	24 g
saturated fat	2 g	carbohydrates	36 g
cholesterol	51 mg	potassium	478 mg
sodium	415 mg		

deliciously healthy dinners

thai-style chicken curry

Prep time: 20 minutes
Cook time: 25 minutes

classic Thai flavors blend together beautifully in this delicious curry; add more green curry paste for a spicy kick

For sauce:

1 Tbsp	peanut oil or vegetable oil
1 Tbsp	ginger, minced (or a 1-inch piece, crushed)
½ Tbsp	garlic, minced (about 1 clove)
¼ C	scallions (green onions), rinsed and chopped
1 Tbsp	lemongrass, minced *(or the zest from 1 lemon: Use a peeler to grate a thin layer of skin off a lemon)*
1 Tbsp	Thai green curry paste
½ C	light coconut milk *(or use a spoon to discard visible layer of fat off the top of an unshaken can of regular coconut milk; then, measure ½ C for recipe)*
1 tsp	honey
1 tsp	lite soy sauce
1 tsp	fish sauce
1 Tbsp	cornstarch
½ C	low-sodium chicken broth

For chicken and vegetables:

1 bag	(12 oz) frozen vegetable stir-fry
12 oz	boneless, skinless chicken breast, cut into thin strips

1. Thaw frozen vegetables in the microwave (or place entire bag in a bowl of hot water for about 10 minutes). Set aside until step 7.

2. For sauce, heat oil in a small saucepan on medium heat. Add ginger, garlic, scallions, and lemongrass, and cook gently until tender, but not brown, about 2–3 minutes.

3. Add curry paste, and cook for an additional 2–3 minutes.

4. Add coconut milk, honey, soy sauce, and fish sauce, and bring to a boil over high heat.

5. In a bowl, mix cornstarch with chicken broth. Add mixture to the saucepan, and return to a boil while stirring constantly.

continued on page 21

thai-style chicken curry (continued)

6. Lower heat to a simmer, and add chicken strips. Simmer gently for 5–8 minutes.

7. Add thawed vegetables, and continue to cook gently with lid on until the vegetables are heated through, an additional 2–3 minutes.

8. Divide into four even portions, each about 3 ounces chicken breast and 1 cup vegetables, and serve.

Tip: Delicious served over rice or Asian-style noodles (soba or udon).

yield: 4 servings

serving size: 3 oz chicken, 1 C vegetables

each serving provides:

calories	207	total fiber	3 g
total fat	7 g	protein	23 g
saturated fat	3 g	carbohydrates	14 g
cholesterol	50 mg	potassium	406 mg
sodium	249 mg		

sweet-and-sour chicken

Prep time: 15 minutes
Cook time: 15 minutes

sweet and sour flavors make a winning combination in this healthier version of a popular Chinese dish

1 bag	(12 oz) frozen vegetable stir-fry
1 Tbsp	peanut oil or vegetable oil
1 Tbsp	ginger, minced
1 Tbsp	garlic, minced (about 2–3 cloves)
1 Tbsp	fresh scallions (green onions), minced
2 Tbsp	rice vinegar
1 Tbsp	Asian hot chili sauce
2 Tbsp	brown sugar
1 Tbsp	cornstarch
1 C	low-sodium chicken broth
12 oz	boneless, skinless chicken breast, cut into thin strips
1 Tbsp	lite soy sauce

1. Thaw frozen vegetables in the microwave (or place entire bag in a bowl of hot water for about 10 minutes). Set aside until step 6.

2. Heat oil in a large wok or sauté pan on medium heat. Add ginger, garlic, and scallions, and stir fry until cooked, but not brown, about 2–3 minutes.

3. Add the rice vinegar, chili sauce, and brown sugar to the pan, and bring to a simmer.

4. In a bowl, mix cornstarch with chicken broth, and add to the pan. Bring to a boil over high heat, stirring constantly. Lower temperature to a gentle simmer.

5. Add chicken, and stir continually for 5–8 minutes.

6. Add vegetables, and mix gently. Simmer with lid on to reheat, about 2 minutes.

7. Add soy sauce, and mix gently.

8. Divide into four even portions, and serve.

Tip: Try serving with a side of steamed rice.

yield: 4 servings

serving size: 3 oz chicken, 1 C vegetables

each serving provides:

calories	221	total fiber	3 g
total fat	6 g	protein	23 g
saturated fat	1 g	carbohydrates	21 g
cholesterol	51 mg	potassium	460 mg
sodium	287 mg		

chicken quesadillas with red and green salsa

Prep time: 30 minutes
Cook time: 10 minutes

this delicious finger food can be served as an appetizer or main-dish meal

For salsa:

4	medium tomatoes, rinsed and diced (about 2 C)
½ C	red onion, diced
1	medium Jalapeno chili pepper, rinsed and split lengthwise—remove seeds and white membrane, and mince (about 2 Tbsp); for less spice, use a green bell pepper
2 Tbsp	lime juice (or about 4 limes)
2 Tbsp	fresh cilantro, rinsed, dried, and chopped *(or substitute 2 tsp dried coriander)*
1 tsp	ground cumin

For quesadillas:

12 oz	boneless, skinless chicken breast, cut into thin strips
4	(10-inch) whole-wheat tortillas
¼ tsp	salt
½ tsp	chili sauce
2 oz	pepper jack cheese, shredded (about ½ C)
1 Tbsp	pine nuts, toasted (optional)
Cooking spray	

1. Preheat oven broiler on high temperature, with the rack 3 inches from heat source.
2. For salsa, combine all ingredients and toss well. Chill in refrigerator for at least 15 minutes. (Salsa can be made up to 1 day in advance and refrigerated.)
3. Cut chicken into thin strips, and place them on a baking sheet coated with cooking spray. Broil for 8–10 minutes.
4. To assemble the quesadillas, place four whole-wheat tortillas on the countertop or table. Top each with one-quarter of the sliced cooked chicken, salt, chili sauce, cheese, and pine nuts (optional).
5. Fold tortillas in half to close, and carefully transfer each to a baking sheet lined with parchment or wax paper.
6. Bake quesadillas at 350 °F for 5–10 minutes or until the cheese is melted.
7. Serve one quesadilla with ½ cup salsa on the side.

Tip: Delicious with a side of fresh grilled corn-on-the-cob.

yield: 4 servings

serving size: 1 quesadilla, ½ C salsa

each serving provides:

calories	339	total fiber	4 g
total fat	11 g	protein	26 g
saturated fat	3 g	carbohydrates	32 g
cholesterol	62 mg	potassium	454 mg
sodium	453 mg		

deliciously healthy dinners

chicken and mushroom fricassee

Prep time: 10 minutes
Cook time: 30 minutes

fat-free sour cream, vegetables, and herbs make this rich and hearty dish guilt free

1 Tbsp	olive oil
1 carton	(10 oz) white button mushrooms, rinsed and quartered
1 C	leeks, split into quarters, then sliced into small squares and rinsed well
1 C	potatoes, peeled and diced
1 C	celery, rinsed and diced
1 C	pearl onions, raw or frozen
3 C	low-sodium chicken broth
1 lb	skinless chicken legs or thighs (4 whole legs, split, or 8 thighs)
2 Tbsp	each fresh herbs (such as parsley and chives), rinsed, dried, and minced (or 2 tsp dried)
1 Tbsp	lemon juice
1 Tbsp	cornstarch
2 Tbsp	fat-free sour cream
½ tsp	salt
¼ tsp	ground black pepper

1. Preheat oven to 350 °F.

2. Heat olive oil in a medium-sized heavy-bottom roasting or braising pan (a large sauté pan with a metal handle will work as well).

3. Add mushrooms to pan, and cook until golden brown, about 3–5 minutes. Add leeks, potatoes, celery, and pearl onions, and continue to cook until the vegetables become soft, about 3–5 additional minutes.

4. Add chicken broth to the pan, and bring to a boil. Add chicken legs to the pan, cover, and place in the heated oven for about 20 minutes or until the chicken legs are tender when pierced with a fork (to a minimum internal temperature of 165 °F).

5. When chicken legs are tender, remove legs from the pan, return the pan to the stovetop, and bring the liquid to a boil. Add herbs and lemon juice.

6. In a bowl, mix the cornstarch with the sour cream, and add to the pan. Bring back to a boil and then remove from the heat.

7. Season with salt and pepper, and pour 1 cup of vegetables and sauce over chicken.

Tip: Try serving over pasta with a side of **Baby Spinach With Golden Raisins and Pine Nuts** (on page 107).

yield: 4 servings

serving size: 1 chicken leg, 1 C vegetables and sauce

each serving provides:

calories	242	total fiber	3 g
total fat	9 g	protein	20 g
saturated fat	2 g	carbohydrates	24 g
cholesterol	42 mg	potassium	807 mg
sodium	430 mg		

deliciously healthy dinners

chicken and celery stir-fry

Prep time: 20 minutes
Cook time: 20 minutes

serve on top of steamed brown rice, and you have a quick, easy, and delicious weeknight meal

1 Tbsp	peanut oil or vegetable oil
1 Tbsp	ginger, minced
1 Tbsp	garlic, minced (about 2–3 cloves)
1 Tbsp	fresh scallions (green onions), rinsed and minced
2 C	celery, rinsed and sliced
1 C	carrots, rinsed and peeled into very thin strips
1 Tbsp	cornstarch
1 C	low-sodium chicken broth
2 Tbsp	rice vinegar
12 oz	boneless, skinless chicken breast, cut into thin strips
1 Tbsp	lite soy sauce
½ Tbsp	sesame oil (optional)
1 Tbsp	sesame seeds, toasted (optional)

1. Heat oil in a large wok or sauté pan. Add ginger, garlic, and scallions, and stir fry briefly until cooked, but not brown, about 30 seconds to 1 minute.
2. Add celery and carrots, and continue to cook gently until the celery begins to soften.
3. In a bowl, mix cornstarch with chicken broth, and add to the pan. Add rice vinegar, and bring to a boil over high heat. Lower temperature to a gentle simmer.
4. Add chicken, and stir continually for 5–8 minutes.
5. Add soy sauce, sesame oil (optional), and sesame seeds (optional), and mix gently.
6. Serve 1 cup chicken stir-fry.

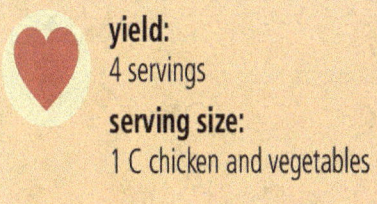

yield: 4 servings

serving size: 1 C chicken and vegetables

each serving provides:

calories	188	total fiber	2 g
total fat	7 g	protein	22 g
saturated fat	2 g	carbohydrates	8 g
cholesterol	51 mg	potassium	370 mg
sodium	237 mg		

oven-crusted chicken breast

Prep time: 20 minutes
Cook time: 20 minutes

a healthy way to fry chicken

For chicken:

4	boneless, skinless chicken breasts (3 oz each)
1	egg white *(or substitute liquid egg white)*
1 C	fat-free evaporated milk
1 C	breadcrumbs
¼ C	rolled oats, crushed; pulse a few times in the food processor or crush between fingers to make smaller pieces
1 C	whole-wheat flour
2 Tbsp	olive oil or vegetable oil

For salad:

2 Tbsp	lemon juice
½ Tbsp	olive oil
4 C	red leaf lettuce, rinsed and dried
1 C	cherry tomatoes, rinsed and halved
¼ tsp	salt
¼ tsp	ground black pepper

Tip: Try serving with a side of oven-roasted potatoes.

1. Preheat oven to 350 °F.

2. Place chicken in a freezer bag with the air squeezed out, and pound each breast down to ½-inch thickness.

3. Combine the egg white and evaporated milk in a bowl, and mix well. In a separate bowl, combine the breadcrumbs and crushed oats, and mix well.

4. Coat the chicken breasts in flour, and shake off the excess. Dip the chicken breasts in the egg and milk mixture, and drain off the excess. Then dip the chicken breasts in the breadcrumb mixture to coat, and shake off the excess. After all chicken breasts have been coated, discard any leftover breading mixture.

5. Heat oil in a large sauté pan. Stir fry the chicken over medium-high heat on one side until golden brown, about 2–3 minutes. Turn carefully, and pan fry the second side for an additional 2–3 minutes or until golden brown. Remove from the pan, and place on paper towels to soak up excess oil. Place on baking sheet, and finish cooking in a 350 °F oven for about 5–8 minutes (to a minimum internal temperature of 165 °F).

6. For the salad, combine lemon juice and olive oil, and mix well to make a dressing. Toss the lettuce leaves and cherry tomatoes with the dressing, salt, and pepper.

7. Serve 1 cup salad with one piece of chicken.

yield: 4 servings

serving size: 3 oz chicken breast, 1 C salad

each serving provides:

calories	264	total fiber	3 g
total fat	11 g	protein	24 g
saturated fat	2 g	carbohydrates	18 g
cholesterol	49 mg	potassium	553 mg
sodium	263 mg		

deliciously healthy dinners

chicken picadillo

Prep time: 15 minutes
Cook time: 25 minutes

this zesty one-pot meal is easy to throw together on a busy weeknight

2 tsp	olive oil
1	large yellow onion, finely chopped
1	medium green bell pepper, rinsed and finely chopped
1	medium red bell pepper, rinsed and finely chopped
1½ Tbsp	garlic, mashed (about 3 cloves)
12 oz	boneless, skinless chicken breast, cut into thin strips
⅓ C	no-salt-added tomato sauce
⅓ C	low-sodium chicken broth
⅓ C	lemon juice
¼ tsp	ground cumin
2	bay leaves
⅓ C	water
¼ C	golden seedless raisins

For garnish:

1 Tbsp	fresh cilantro, rinsed, dried, and chopped *(or substitute 1 tsp dried coriander)*
1 Tbsp	capers, drained
2 Tbsp	green olives, chopped

1. Heat olive oil in a large sauté pan over medium heat. Add the onion, bell peppers, and garlic, and sauté until vegetables are soft, about 5 minutes.

2. Add the chicken, and stir fry for another 5–10 minutes, until chicken is no longer pink inside.

3. Add the tomato sauce, chicken broth, lemon juice, cumin, bay leaves, water, and raisins to the vegetables and chicken.

4. Cover the pan, and reduce the heat. Simmer for 10 minutes.

5. Remove the bay leaves, and garnish with fresh cilantro, capers, and green olives, and serve.

Tip: Serve with brown rice and black beans.

yield: 6 servings
serving size: ¾ C chicken and vegetables

each serving provides:

calories	162	total fiber	2 g
total fat	5 g	protein	18 g
saturated fat	1 g	carbohydrates	13 g
cholesterol	46 mg	potassium	380 mg
sodium	133 mg		

deliciously healthy dinners

chicken ratatouille

Prep time: 15 minutes
Cook time: 20 minutes

it may be hard to say "ratatouille" (pronounced rat-uh-TOO-ee), but this one-dish recipe will show you that it's very easy to eat

1 Tbsp	vegetable oil
12 oz	boneless, skinless chicken breast, cut into thin strips
2	zucchini, about 7 inches long, unpeeled, thinly sliced
1	small eggplant, peeled, cut into 1-inch cubes
1	medium onion, thinly sliced
1	medium green bell pepper, rinsed and cut into 1-inch pieces
½ lb	fresh mushrooms, rinsed and sliced
1 can	(14½ oz) whole peeled tomatoes, chopped
½ Tbsp	garlic, minced (about 1 clove)
1½ tsp	dried basil, crushed
1 Tbsp	fresh parsley, rinsed, dried, and minced
⅛ tsp	ground black pepper

1. Heat oil in a large nonstick pan. Add chicken, and sauté for about 3 minutes or until lightly browned.

2. Add zucchini, eggplant, onion, green pepper, and mushrooms. Cook for about 15 minutes, stirring occasionally.

3. Add tomatoes, garlic, basil, parsley, and black pepper. Stir and continue to cook for about 5 minutes. Serve warm.

Tip: Serve with a side of whole-wheat pasta.

yield: 4 servings

serving size: 1½ C chicken and vegetables

each serving provides:

calories	266	total fiber	6 g
total fat	8 g	protein	30 g
saturated fat	2 g	carbohydrates	21 g
cholesterol	66 mg	potassium	1,148 mg
sodium	253 mg		

deliciously healthy dinners

asian-style chicken wraps

Prep time: 15 minutes
Cook time: 20 minutes

delicious on their own, or try serving with a side of **Sunshine Rice** (on page 126)

For sauce:

1	small Jalapeno chili pepper, rinsed and split lengthwise—remove seeds and white membrane, and mince (about 1 Tbsp); for less spice, use green bell pepper
1 Tbsp	garlic, minced (about 2–3 cloves)
3 Tbsp	brown sugar or honey
½ C	water
½ Tbsp	fish sauce
2 Tbsp	lime juice (or about 4 limes)

For chicken:

1 Tbsp	peanut oil or vegetable oil
1 Tbsp	ginger, minced
1 Tbsp	garlic, minced (about 2–3 cloves)
12 oz	boneless, skinless chicken breast, cut into thin strips
1 Tbsp	lite soy sauce
1 Tbsp	sesame oil (optional)
1 Tbsp	sesame seeds (optional)

For wrap:

1	(small) head red leaf lettuce, rinsed, dried, and separated into single leaves large enough to create wrap
8	fresh basil leaves, whole, rinsed and dried
2 C	bok choy or Asian cabbage, rinsed and shredded

1. To prepare the sauce, add all ingredients to a saucepan, and bring to a boil over high heat. Remove from heat, and let sit in hot saucepan for 3–5 minutes. Chill in refrigerator for about 15 minutes or until cold.

2. Prepare the chicken by heating oil in a large wok or sauté pan. Add ginger and garlic, and stir fry briefly until cooked but not brown, about 30 seconds to 1 minute.

continued on page 31

asian-style chicken wraps (continued)

3. Add chicken, and continue to stir fry for 5–8 minutes.
4. Add soy sauce, sesame oil (optional), and sesame seeds (optional), and return to a boil. Remove from the heat, and cover with lid to hold warm in hot sauté pan.
5. Assemble each wrap: Place one large red lettuce leaf on a plate, then add ½ cup chicken stir-fry, 1 basil leaf, and ¼ cup shredded cabbage and fold together. Serve two wraps with ¼ cup sauce.

yield:
4 servings

serving size:
2 wraps, ¼ C sauce

each serving provides:

calories	242	total fiber	3 g
total fat	10 g	protein	21 g
saturated fat	2 g	carbohydrates	17 g
cholesterol	47 mg	potassium	636 mg
sodium	393 mg		

cornbread-crusted turkey

Prep time: 20 minutes
Cook time: 20 minutes

not just for Thanksgiving—enjoy this hearty turkey dinner any time of year

1 C	low-fat buttermilk
1 Tbsp	Dijon mustard
4	skinless turkey fillets (3 oz each)
	4- by 4-inch square prepared cornbread (about 1 C crumbs) (See **Good-for-You Cornbread** on page 119)
1	egg white *(or substitute liquid egg white)*
1 C	low-sodium chicken broth
1 Tbsp	cornstarch
1 lb	frozen baby carrots
1 Tbsp	fresh sage, rinsed, dried, and chopped (or 1 tsp dried)
1 Tbsp	butter

1. Preheat oven to 350 °F.

2. Combine buttermilk and Dijon mustard. Mix well.

3. Add turkey fillets to buttermilk mixture to marinate for 5–10 minutes while preparing cornbread.

4. Grind cornbread in a food processor, or use your fingers to make coarse crumbs. Place breadcrumbs on a baking sheet, and dry in a 300 °F oven or toaster oven for 4–5 minutes. Do not brown.

5. Pour breadcrumbs into a dry, shallow dish. Put egg white in a separate bowl.

6. Remove turkey from the buttermilk, and dip each fillet first in the egg white and then in the cornbread crumbs to coat. Be sure to discard leftover buttermilk mixture and cornbread crumbs.

7. Place breaded turkey fillets on a baking sheet, and bake for 10–15 minutes (to a minimum internal temperature of 165 °F).

8. While the turkey is cooking, combine chicken broth, cornstarch, carrots, sage, and butter in a medium saucepan. Bring to a boil over high heat, stirring occasionally. Lower temperature to a simmer.

continued on page 33

cornbread-crusted turkey (continued)

9. Simmer gently for about 5 minutes, or until the butter is melted, the sauce is thick, and the carrots are warm.

10. Serve each 3-ounce turkey fillet with 1 cup of carrots and sauce mixture.

Tip: Try serving with a baked or roasted sweet potato.

yield: 4 servings

serving size: 3 oz turkey, 1 C carrots and sauce mixture

each serving provides:

calories	285	total fiber	3 g
total fat	6 g	protein	29 g
saturated fat	3 g	carbohydrates	29 g
cholesterol	48 mg	potassium	378 mg
sodium	420 mg		

deliciously healthy dinners

turkey club burger

Prep time: 20 minutes
Cook time: 20 minutes

lighten up your traditional hamburger with lean ground turkey—less saturated fat, without less flavor

For turkey burger:

12 oz	99 percent fat-free ground turkey
½ C	scallions (green onions), rinsed and sliced
¼ tsp	ground black pepper
1	large egg
1 Tbsp	olive oil

For spread:

2 Tbsp	light mayonnaise
1 Tbsp	Dijon mustard

For toppings:

4 oz	spinach or arugula, rinsed and dried
4 oz	portabella mushroom, rinsed, grilled or broiled, and sliced (optional)
4	whole-wheat hamburger buns

1. Preheat oven broiler on high temperature (with the rack 3 inches from heat source) or grill on medium-high heat.

2. To prepare burgers, combine ground turkey, scallions, pepper, and egg, and mix well. Form into ½- to ¾-inch thick patties, and coat each lightly with olive oil.

3. Broil or grill burgers for about 7–9 minutes on each side (to a minimum internal temperature of 160 °F).

4. Combine mayonnaise and mustard to make a spread.

5. Assemble ¾ tablespoon spread, 1 ounce spinach or arugula, several slices of grilled portabella mushroom (optional), and one burger on each bun.

Tip: Try it with a side of **Grilled Romaine Lettuce With Caesar Dressing** (on page 105).

Hint: To grill portabella mushrooms, scrape off the gills from underneath the mushroom caps. Lightly coat with olive oil, and grill or broil for 2–3 minutes on each side or until tender. Slice and set aside until burgers are ready.

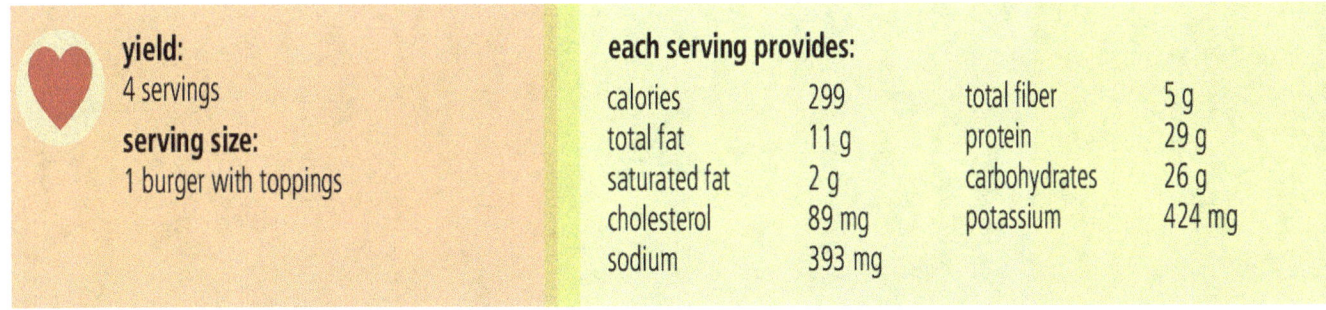

yield:
4 servings

serving size:
1 burger with toppings

each serving provides:

calories	299	total fiber	5 g
total fat	11 g	protein	29 g
saturated fat	2 g	carbohydrates	26 g
cholesterol	89 mg	potassium	424 mg
sodium	393 mg		

turkey mole

Prep time: 15 minutes
Cook time: 30 minutes

mole is a classic Latin sauce, made with cocoa and spices

For sauce:

1 Tbsp	chili powder
1 tsp	ground black pepper
⅛ tsp	ground cloves
⅛ tsp	ground allspice
1 Tbsp	sesame seeds (reserve 1 tsp for garnish) (optional)
2 Tbsp	canola oil, divided into two 1-Tbsp portions
½ Tbsp	garlic, minced (about 1 clove)
½ C	onion, chopped
1 C	canned no-salt-added diced tomatoes
1 tsp	fresh oregano, rinsed, dried, and chopped (or ¼ tsp dried)
1 Tbsp	cocoa powder
1 C	low-sodium chicken broth

For turkey:

12 oz	turkey fillets, boneless and skinless (about 4 pieces)
½ tsp	salt
½ tsp	ground black pepper

1. Preheat grill pan or oven broiler (with the rack 3 inches from heat source) on high temperature.

2. To prepare the sauce, add chili powder, pepper, cloves, allspice, and sesame seeds (optional) to a saucepan, and toast on medium heat for 2 minutes.

3. Add 1 tablespoon canola oil. Sauté garlic on medium to medium-high heat for 30 seconds to 1 minute.

4. Add onion, and sauté until cooked but not brown, about 2–3 minutes.

5. Add tomatoes, oregano, cocoa powder, and chicken broth, and bring to a boil over high heat. Simmer for 8–10 minutes.

6. Remove from the heat, and let cool to room temperature. Puree the sauce in a blender until smooth. Return sauce to the pan, and reheat slowly (or keep sauce warm on stovetop).

7. To prepare the turkey, coat the fillets with 1 tablespoon canola oil and season with salt and pepper.

continued on page 37

turkey mole (continued)

8. Broil turkey in preheated oven or grill for 3–5 minutes on each side or until the turkey is fully cooked (to a minimum internal temperature of 165 °F).

9. Serve one piece of turkey with ½ cup of the warm mole sauce.

Tip: Try serving with rice and **Baby Spinach With Golden Raisins and Pine Nuts** (on page 107).

yield: 4 servings

serving size: 1 turkey fillet, ½ C sauce

each serving provides:

calories	217	total fiber	2 g
total fat	9 g	protein	24 g
saturated fat	1 g	carbohydrates	9 g
cholesterol	53 mg	potassium	419 mg
sodium	421 mg		

20-minute chicken creole

Prep time: 15 minutes
Cook time: 20 minutes

this quick Southern-style dish contains no added fat and very little added salt in its spicy tomato sauce

12 oz	boneless, skinless chicken breast, cut into thin strips
1 C	canned whole peeled tomatoes, chopped
1 C	chili sauce (look for lowest sodium version)
1½ C	green bell pepper, rinsed and chopped
1½ C	celery, rinsed and chopped
¼ C	onion, chopped
1 Tbsp	garlic, minced (about 2–3 cloves)
1 Tbsp	fresh basil, rinsed, dried, and chopped (or 1 tsp dried)
1 Tbsp	fresh parsley, rinsed, dried, and chopped (or 1 tsp dried)
¼ tsp	crushed red pepper
¼ tsp	salt
Cooking spray	

1. Spray sauté pan with cooking spray. Preheat over high heat.
2. Cook chicken in hot sauté pan, stirring for 3–5 minutes. Reduce heat.
3. Add tomatoes with juice, chili sauce, green pepper, celery, onion, garlic, basil, parsley, crushed red pepper, and salt. Bring to a boil over high heat, and then reduce heat to simmer.
4. Simmer, covered, for 10 minutes.

Tip: Delicious served over rice.

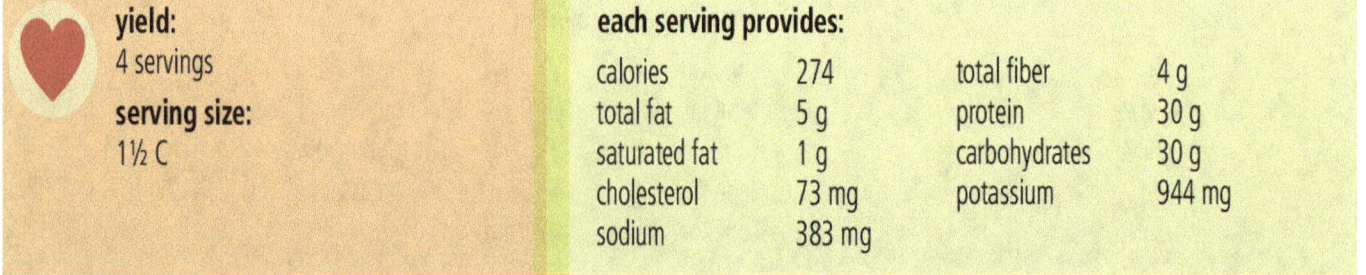

yield: 4 servings
serving size: 1½ C

each serving provides:

calories	274	total fiber	4 g
total fat	5 g	protein	30 g
saturated fat	1 g	carbohydrates	30 g
cholesterol	73 mg	potassium	944 mg
sodium	383 mg		

grilled tuna with chickpea and spinach salad

Prep time: 25 minutes
Cook time: 20 minutes

tuna is a sturdy fish that is easy to grill or broil

1 Tbsp	olive or canola oil
1 Tbsp	garlic, minced (about 2–3 cloves)
2 Tbsp	lemon juice
1 Tbsp	oregano, minced (or 1 tsp dried)
12 oz	tuna steaks, cut into 4 portions (3 oz each)

For salad:

½ can	(15½ oz) low-sodium chickpeas (or garbanzo beans), drained and rinsed
½ bag	(10 oz) leaf spinach, rinsed and dried
1 Tbsp	lemon juice
1	medium tomato, rinsed and cut into wedges
⅛ tsp	salt
⅛ tsp	ground black pepper

1. Preheat grill pan or oven broiler (with the rack 3 inches from heat source) on high temperature.
2. Combine oil, garlic, lemon juice, and oregano, and brush over tuna steaks. Marinate for 5–10 minutes.
3. Meanwhile, combine all salad ingredients. (Salad can be made up to 2 hours in advance and refrigerated.)
4. Grill or broil tuna on high heat for 3–4 minutes on each side until the flesh is opaque and separates easily with a fork (to a minimum internal temperature of 145 °F).
5. Serve one tuna steak over 1 cup of mixed salad.

Tip: Try with a side of **Quinoa With Paprika and Cumin** (on page 118).

Note: If you can't find beans labeled "low-sodium," compare the Nutrition Facts panels to find the beans with the lowest amount of sodium. Rinsing can help further reduce the sodium level.

yield: 4 servings

serving size: 1 tuna steak, 1 C salad

each serving provides:

calories	282	total fiber	5 g
total fat	10 g	protein	31 g
saturated fat	2 g	carbohydrates	15 g
cholesterol	42 mg	potassium	874 mg
sodium	418 mg		

deliciously healthy dinners

baja-style salmon tacos

Prep time: 20 minutes
Cook time: 15 minutes

fun finger food for a hot summer night

12 oz	salmon fillet, cut into 4 portions (3 oz each)
4	(8-inch) whole-wheat tortillas

For taco filling:

1 C	green cabbage (about ¼ head), rinsed and shredded
1 tsp	lime juice
1 tsp	honey
½ C	red onion, thinly sliced *(or substitute white onion)*
1	medium Jalapeno chili pepper, rinsed and split lengthwise—remove seeds and white membrane, and mince (about 2 Tbsp); for less spice, use green bell pepper
1 tsp	fresh cilantro, minced *(or substitute ½ tsp ground coriander)*

For marinade:

½ Tbsp	corn oil or other vegetable oil
1 Tbsp	lime juice
2 tsp	chili powder
½ tsp	ground cumin
½ tsp	ground coriander
¼ tsp	salt

1. Preheat grill or oven broiler (with the rack 3 inches from heat source) on high temperature.
2. Prepare taco filling by combining all ingredients. Let stand for 10–15 minutes to blend the flavors.
3. To prepare the marinade, combine the oil, lime juice, chili powder, cumin, coriander, and salt in a bowl.
4. Place salmon fillets in a flat dish with sides. Pour marinade evenly over fillets.
5. Place salmon fillets on grill or broiler. Cook for 3–4 minutes on each side, until fish flakes easily with a fork in the thickest part (to a minimum internal temperature of 145 °F). Remove from the heat and set aside for 2–3 minutes. Cut into strips.
6. To make each taco, fill one tortilla with ¾ cup filling and one salmon fillet.

Tip: Try serving with a tomato cucumber salad drizzled with light vinaigrette.

yield: 4 servings
serving size: 1 taco

each serving provides:

calories	325	total fiber	4 g
total fat	11 g	protein	24 g
saturated fat	1 g	carbohydrates	29 g
cholesterol	54 mg	potassium	614 mg
sodium	395 mg		

spanish-style shrimp stew

Prep time: 20 minutes
Cook time: 25 minutes

enjoy this Mediterranean-flavored seafood stew

1 Tbsp	olive oil
1 Tbsp	garlic, minced (about 2–3 cloves)
1 C	fennel (about 1 bulb, outer layers removed), rinsed and diced (*or substitute leek or onion*)
2 cans	(14½ oz each) no-salt-added diced tomatoes
1 C	low-sodium chicken broth
2 lb	new (red) potatoes, rinsed and quartered (about 2 C)
12 oz	large shrimp, peeled and deveined (about 24 pieces)
2 Tbsp	fresh oregano, rinsed, dried, and chopped (or 2 tsp dried)
2 Tbsp	lemon juice
2 Tbsp	fresh basil, rinsed, dried, and chopped (or 2 tsp dried)
¼ tsp	salt
¼ tsp	ground black pepper

1. Heat olive oil in a large sauté pan. Add garlic and fennel, and cook on medium heat, stirring often, until the fennel pieces begin to soften, about 5–7 minutes.

2. Add tomatoes, chicken broth, and potatoes, and bring to a boil. Lower temperature to a gentle simmer, and cook until the potatoes begin to soften, about 10 minutes.

3. Add shrimp, oregano, lemon juice, and basil, and mix gently. Continue to simmer until the shrimp are pink and fully cooked, about 5 minutes (to a minimum internal temperature of 145 °F).

4. Add salt and pepper.

5. Serve 1½ cups stew (each serving to include about six shrimp).

Tip: Delicious over rice or with a green salad and crispy and crusty bread (broiled with garlic) to soak up the sauce.

yield: 4 servings

serving size: 1½ C stew

each serving provides:

calories	211	total fiber	4 g
total fat	5 g	protein	18 g
saturated fat	1 g	carbohydrates	25 g
cholesterol	126 mg	potassium	276 mg
sodium	375 mg		

braised cod with leeks

Prep time: 15 minutes
Cook time: 25 minutes

a simple, but elegant, weeknight meal

1 Tbsp	butter
2 C	leeks, split lengthwise, sliced thin, and rinsed well
3	medium carrots, rinsed, peeled, and cut into thin sticks
4	new (red) potatoes, rinsed and sliced into ½-inch thick circles
2 C	low-sodium chicken broth
2 Tbsp	fresh parsley, rinsed, dried, and chopped (or 2 tsp dried)
12 oz	cod fillets, cut into 4 portions (3 oz each)
½ tsp	salt
¼ tsp	ground black pepper

1. Heat butter in a large sauté pan. Add leeks and carrots, and cook gently for 3–5 minutes, stirring often, until the vegetables begin to soften.

2. Add potatoes, chicken broth, parsley, and salt and pepper, and bring to a boil over high heat. Reduce heat and simmer gently until the vegetables are just tender, about 10–12 minutes.

3. Add cod fillets, and cover with a tight-fitting lid. Continue cooking over low heat for an additional 5 minutes or until the fish is white and flakes easily with a fork in the thickest part (to a minimum internal temperature of 145 °F).

4. Serve each cod fillet with 1½ cups broth and vegetables.

Tip: Delicious with **Asparagus With Lemon Sauce** (on page 103).

yield:
4 servings

serving size:
3 oz cod, 1½ C broth and vegetables

each serving provides:

calories	158	total fiber	3 g
total fat	4 g	protein	17 g
saturated fat	2 g	carbohydrates	13 g
cholesterol	42 mg	potassium	476 mg
sodium	437 mg		

deliciously healthy dinners

baked red snapper with zesty tomato sauce

Prep time: 10 minutes
Cook time: 40 minutes

traditional Mediterranean-style fish with tomatoes and peppers

For fish:

12 oz	fillets of red snapper or bass, cut into 4 portions (3 oz each)
1 Tbsp	olive oil
½ tsp	salt
¼ tsp	ground black pepper

For tomato sauce:

1 Tbsp	olive oil
1	red bell pepper, rinsed and cut into ¼-inch sticks
1	green bell pepper, rinsed and cut into ¼-inch sticks
1 C	canned no-salt-added diced tomatoes
2 C	canned no-salt-added tomato sauce
1 Tbsp	fresh oregano, rinsed, dried, and chopped (or 1 tsp dried)
1 Tbsp	fresh basil, rinsed, dried, and chopped (or 1 tsp dried)
1 Tbsp	fresh parsley, rinsed, dried, and chopped (or 1 tsp dried)

1. Preheat oven to 350 °F. Rinse fish fillets in cold water. Pat dry with paper towels. Coat each fillet with olive oil and season with salt and pepper.

2. Place fish fillets on a baking sheet, and bake for 25–30 minutes or until fish is white and flakes easily with a fork in the thickest part (to a minimum internal temperature of 145 °F).

3. For sauce, heat olive oil in a medium-sized saucepan.

4. Add bell peppers, and cook gently until they are still firm, but tender, about 3–5 minutes.

5. Add tomatoes and tomato sauce, and bring to a boil over high heat. Reduce heat and simmer for 10–15 minutes or until the tomatoes are soft. Add oregano, basil, and parsley, and simmer for an additional 2–3 minutes. Remove sauce from the heat and set aside.

6. When the fish is done (see step 2), remove from the oven.

7. Serve each 3-ounce fillet with 1 cup of sauce.

Tip: Delicious served with **Pesto Baked Polenta** (on page 125).

yield:
4 servings

serving size:
3 oz fillet, 1 C sauce

each serving provides:

calories	213	total fiber	4 g
total fat	8 g	protein	20 g
saturated fat	1 g	carbohydrates	15 g
cholesterol	30 mg	potassium	910 mg
sodium	365 mg		

teriyaki-glazed salmon with stir-fried vegetables

Prep time: 20 minutes
Cook time: 15 minutes

a fresh and flavorful Asian-style dish that is as easy to make as it is colorful

For salmon:

2 Tbsp	light teriyaki sauce
¼ C	mirin (or sweet rice wine)
2 Tbsp	rice vinegar
2 Tbsp	scallions (green onions), rinsed and minced
1½ Tbsp	ginger, minced (or 1 tsp ground)
12 oz	salmon fillets, cut into 4 portions (3 oz each)

For vegetables:

1 bag	(12 oz) frozen vegetable stir-fry
½ Tbsp	peanut oil or vegetable oil
½ Tbsp	garlic, minced (about 1 clove)
1 Tbsp	ginger, minced (or 1 tsp ground)
1 Tbsp	scallions (green onions), rinsed and minced
1 Tbsp	lite soy sauce

1. Thaw frozen vegetables in the microwave (or place entire bag in a bowl of hot water for about 10 minutes). Set aside until step 7.

2. Preheat oven to 350 °F.

3. Combine teriyaki sauce, mirin, rice vinegar, scallions, and ginger. Mix well. Pour over salmon, and marinate for 10–15 minutes.

4. Remove salmon from the marinade, and discard unused portion.

5. Place salmon on a baking sheet, and bake for 10–15 minutes or until fish flakes easily with a fork in the thickest part (to a minimum internal temperature of 145 °F).

6. Meanwhile, heat oil in a large wok or sauté pan. Add garlic, ginger, and scallions, and cook gently but do not brown, about 30 seconds to 1 minute.

7. Add vegetables, and continue to stir fry for 2–3 minutes or until heated through. Add soy sauce.

8. Serve one piece of salmon with 1 cup of vegetables.

Tip: Try serving with steamed rice or Asian-style noodles (soba or udon).

yield:
4 servings

serving size:
3 oz salmon, 1 C vegetables

each serving provides:

calories	253	total fiber	3 g
total fat	11 g	protein	21 g
saturated fat	2 g	carbohydrates	16 g
cholesterol	50 mg	potassium	584 mg
sodium	202 mg		

deliciously healthy dinners

red snapper provencal

Prep time: 20 minutes
Cook time: 20 minutes

a crispy, Mediterranean-style fish fillet with tomatoes, olives, and anchovies

2 Tbsp	olive oil
12 oz	red snapper, bass, or tilapia fillets, cut into 4 portions (3 oz each)
1½ Tbsp	garlic, minced (about 3–4 cloves)
½ C	low-sodium chicken broth
1 C	canned no-salt-added diced tomatoes
¼ C	black olives, sliced
½ Tbsp	anchovy paste (optional)
2 Tbsp	fresh basil, chopped (or ½ Tbsp dried)
¼ tsp	ground black pepper

1. Heat olive oil in a large, heavy-bottom sauté pan.
2. Add fillets, and sauté over high heat for 4–5 minutes on each side or until each side is golden brown and the fish flakes easily with a fork in the thickest part (to a minimum internal temperature of 145° F).
3. Remove fillets from the pan, cover to keep warm, and set aside. Drain excess fat from pan, but do not clean.
4. Add garlic to sauté pan, and cook for about 30 seconds, until it begins to soften. Do not brown.
5. Add chicken broth to the pan, and bring to a boil over high heat. Add remaining ingredients, and return to a boil. Lower heat and simmer for 5 minutes.
6. Serve each fish fillet with ½ cup of sauce.

Tip: Try serving with a side of steamed broccoli and crusty bread or **Whole-Wheat Bow Tie Pasta With Puttanesca Sauce** (on page 73).

yield: 4 servings
serving size: 3 oz fish, ½ C sauce

each serving provides:

calories	216	total fiber	2 g
total fat	10 g	protein	25 g
saturated fat	2 g	carbohydrates	6 g
cholesterol	43 mg	potassium	518 mg
sodium	341 mg		

deliciously healthy dinners

asian-style steamed salmon

Prep time: 15 minutes
Cook time: 10 minutes

enjoy this simple, fast dish any weeknight

1 C	low-sodium chicken broth
½ C	shiitake mushroom caps, rinsed and sliced *(or substitute dried shiitake mushrooms)*
2 Tbsp	fresh ginger, minced (or 2 tsp ground)
¼ C	scallions (green onions), rinsed and chopped
1 Tbsp	lite soy sauce
1 Tbsp	sesame oil (optional)
12 oz	salmon fillet, cut into 4 portions (3 oz each)

1. Combine chicken broth, mushroom caps, ginger, scallions, soy sauce, and sesame oil (optional) in a large, shallow sauté pan. Bring to a boil over high heat, then lower heat and simmer for 2–3 minutes.

2. Add salmon fillets, and cover with a tight-fitting lid. Cook gently over low heat for 4–5 minutes or until the salmon flakes easily with a fork in the thickest part (to a minimum internal temperature of 145 °F).

3. Serve one piece of salmon with ¼ cup of broth.

Tip: Try it with a side of **Sunshine Rice** (on page 126).

yield: 4 servings

serving size: 3 oz salmon, ¼ C broth

each serving provides:

calories	175	total fiber	1 g
total fat	9 g	protein	19 g
saturated fat	2 g	carbohydrates	4 g
cholesterol	48 mg	potassium	487 mg
sodium	208 mg		

deliciously healthy dinners

baked salmon dijon

Prep time: 10 minutes
Cook time: 20 minutes

this salmon entree is easy to make and will be enjoyed by the whole family

1 C	fat-free sour cream
2 tsp	dried dill
3 Tbsp	scallions (green onions), rinsed and finely chopped
2 Tbsp	Dijon mustard
2 Tbsp	lemon juice
1½ lb	salmon fillet, cut into 6 portions (4 oz each)
½ tsp	garlic powder
½ tsp	ground black pepper
Cooking spray	

1. Preheat oven to 400 °F.
2. Whisk sour cream, dill, scallions, mustard, and lemon juice in a small bowl to blend.
3. Lightly coat baking sheet with cooking spray.
4. Place salmon, skin side down, on the prepared baking sheet. Sprinkle with garlic powder and pepper, then spread with sauce.
5. Bake salmon fillets until each is opaque in the center and flakes easily with a fork in the thickest part, about 20 minutes (to a minimum internal temperature of 145 °F).
6. Serve immediately.

Tip: Pairs nicely with steamed broccoli and **Parmesan Rice and Pasta Pilaf** (on page 123).

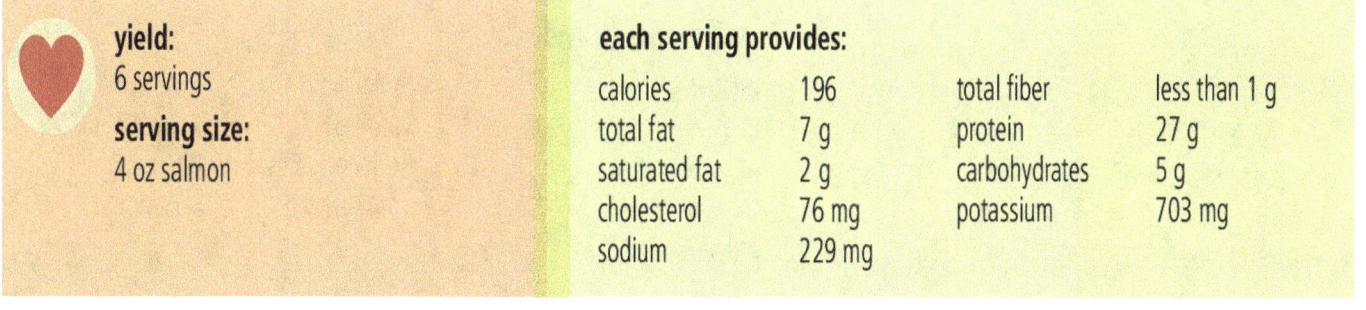

yield: 6 servings
serving size: 4 oz salmon

each serving provides:

calories	196	total fiber	less than 1 g
total fat	7 g	protein	27 g
saturated fat	2 g	carbohydrates	5 g
cholesterol	76 mg	potassium	703 mg
sodium	229 mg		

fish veronique

Prep time: 5 minutes
Cook time: 20 minutes

here's a trick to treat the taste buds—remove the fat from the chicken broth and add low-fat milk to get a healthy sauce that tastes rich and looks creamy

12 oz	white fish (such as cod, sole, or turbot), cut into 4 portions (3 oz each)
¼ tsp	salt
⅛ tsp	ground black pepper
¼ C	dry white wine
¼ C	chicken broth; skim fat from the top
1 Tbsp	lemon juice
1 Tbsp	soft tub margarine
2 Tbsp	flour
¾ C	low-fat (1 percent) or fat-free milk
½ C	seedless grapes, rinsed
Cooking spray	

1. Preheat oven to 350 °F.
2. Spray a 10- by 6-inch baking dish with cooking spray. Place fish in dish, and sprinkle with salt and pepper.
3. Mix wine, chicken broth, and lemon juice in a small bowl, and pour over fish.
4. Cover and bake at 350 °F for 15 minutes.
5. Meanwhile, melt margarine in a small saucepan. Remove from heat and blend in flour. Gradually add milk. Return to stovetop and cook over moderately low heat, stirring constantly, until thickened.
6. Remove fish from oven, and pour liquid from baking dish into "cream" sauce, stirring until blended. Pour sauce over fish and sprinkle with grapes.
7. Broil about 3 inches from heat for 5 minutes or until sauce starts to brown (and fish reaches a minimum internal temperature of 145 °F).
8. Serve one fillet with sauce.

Tip: Try serving with a side of steamed spinach and roasted potatoes.

yield: 4 servings
serving size: 3 oz fillet with sauce

each serving provides:

calories	166	total fiber	less than 1 g
total fat	2 g	protein	24 g
saturated fat	1 g	carbohydrates	9 g
cholesterol	61 mg	potassium	453 mg
sodium	343 mg		

deliciously healthy dinners

pork mignons with french applesauce

Prep time: 15 minutes
Cook time: 25 minutes

consider doubling the sauce to serve over whole-wheat pancakes, or eat all alone for dessert

1	pair pork tenderloins (about 2 lb)
¼ tsp	salt
⅛ tsp	ground black pepper
2	medium apples, rinsed and cored, but not peeled (try Golden Delicious or Rome)
2 Tbsp	dark seedless raisins
2 Tbsp	walnuts, broken into coarse pieces
½ tsp	cinnamon
Cooking spray	

1. Preheat oven broiler on high temperature, with the rack 3 inches from heat source.

2. Cover broiler pan with aluminum foil for easy cleanup. Spray foil lightly with cooking spray. Set aside.

3. Cut 8 slices (pork rounds), each 1½ inches thick, from the center of the pair of pork tenderloins. Refrigerate or freeze the ends for another use. Place pork rounds on the foil-covered broiler pan. Sprinkle with salt and pepper. Set aside a few minutes while broiler heats.

4. Meanwhile, heat ½ cup water to boiling in a medium nonstick pan. Slice cored apples from top to bottom in ¼-inch wide pieces. Add apples, raisins, walnuts, and cinnamon to boiling water. Reduce heat to medium. Cover. Simmer, stirring occasionally, until apples are soft and easily pierced with a fork. Set aside until pork is cooked.

5. Broil pork for 5–10 minutes per side (to a minimum internal temperature of 160 °F).

6. To serve, place two pork rounds on each dinner plate. Top with one-fourth of the applesauce.

Tip: Delicious with rice and a side of **Cinnamon-Glazed Baby Carrots** (on page 113).

yield: 4 servings
serving size: 2 pork rounds, ½ C applesauce

each serving provides:

calories	250	total fiber	3 g
total fat	9 g	protein	26 g
saturated fat	3 g	carbohydrates	15 g
cholesterol	80 mg	potassium	513 mg
sodium	200 mg		

deliciously healthy dinners

pork chops in warm cherry sauce

Prep time: 10 minutes
Cook time: 20 minutes

the rich, savory sauce makes this an elegant dish

4	bone-in center-cut pork chops (about 5 oz each)
¼ tsp	salt
⅛ tsp	ground black pepper
2 tsp	olive oil, divided into 1½ tsp and ½ tsp portions
1 C	onion, diced
1 C	dry red wine
1 tsp	dried tarragon
1 C	dried cherries, either sweet Bing or tart *(or substitute another dried fruit such as raisins, figs, or prunes)*

1. Trim visible fat from pork chops. Sprinkle with salt and pepper.
2. In a large nonstick pan, warm 1½ teaspoons of oil over high heat. When pan is hot, brown chops on both sides, about 2 minutes per side. Remove chops from pan. Set aside.
3. Over medium heat, add remaining ½ teaspoon of oil and diced onion. Cook and stir until onion softens, about 5 minutes.
4. Add red wine. Cook and stir 1 minute to loosen the flavorful brown bits and mix them into the sauce.
5. Add tarragon and cherries. Cook and stir 1 minute to blend.
6. Return pork chops and any juices to pan. Cover. Simmer 9 minutes to thicken sauce and until pork chops are fully cooked (to a minimum internal temperature of 160 °F).
7. Serve immediately.

Tip: Try serving over a whole grain such as **Kasha With Bell Pepper Confetti** (on page 122) and **Cinnamon-Glazed Baby Carrots** (on page 113).

yield: 4 servings
serving size: 5 oz pork, ¼ C cherry sauce

each serving provides:

calories	374	total fiber	4 g
total fat	7 g	protein	34 g
saturated fat	2 g	carbohydrates	31 g
cholesterol	98 mg	potassium	655 mg
sodium	237 mg		

baked pork chops

Prep time: 10 minutes
Cook time: 35 minutes

you can really sink your chops into these—they're made spicy and moist with egg whites, evaporated milk, and a lively blend of herbs

6	lean center-cut pork chops, ½-inch thick*
1	egg white *(or substitute liquid egg white)*
1 C	fat-free evaporated milk
¾ C	cornflake crumbs
¼ C	breadcrumbs
4 tsp	paprika
2 tsp	oregano
¾ tsp	chili powder
½ tsp	garlic powder
½ tsp	ground black pepper
⅛ tsp	cayenne pepper
⅛ tsp	dry mustard
½ tsp	salt
Cooking spray	

1. Preheat oven to 375 °F.
2. Trim fat from pork chops.
3. Beat together egg white and evaporated milk. Place pork chops in milk mixture, and let stand for 5 minutes, turning once.
4. Meanwhile, mix cornflake crumbs, breadcrumbs, spices, and salt.
5. Spray cooking spray on 13- by 9-inch baking pan.
6. Remove pork chops from milk mixture, and coat thoroughly with crumb mixture.
7. Place pork chops in pan, and bake at 375 °F for 20 minutes. Turn chops and bake for an additional 15 minutes until pork is fully cooked (to a minimum internal temperature of 160 °F).
8. Serve immediately.

Tip: Try with baked potatoes and **Roasted Beets With Orange Sauce** (on page 109).

* Also try this recipe with boneless, skinless chicken or turkey parts, or fish—bake for just 20 minutes.

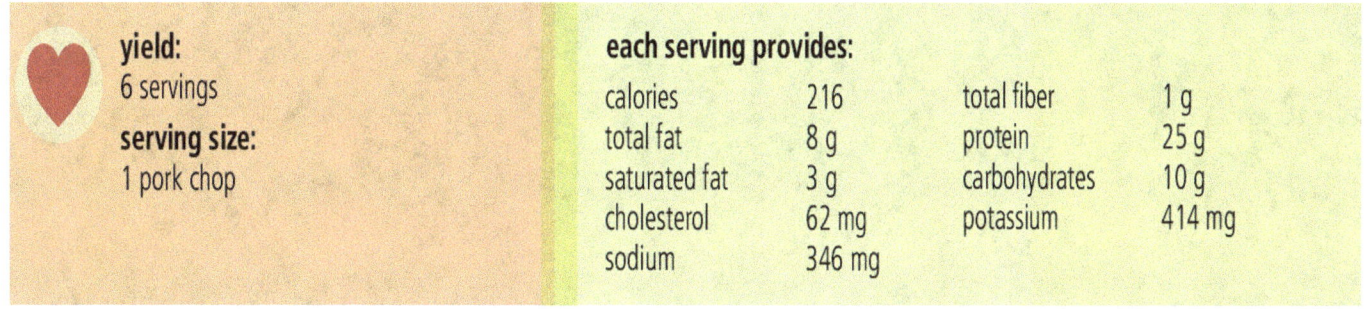

yield: 6 servings
serving size: 1 pork chop

each serving provides:

calories	216	total fiber	1 g
total fat	8 g	protein	25 g
saturated fat	3 g	carbohydrates	10 g
cholesterol	62 mg	potassium	414 mg
sodium	346 mg		

grilled pork tenderloin with asian sauce

Prep time: 15 minutes
Cook time: 30 minutes

fish sauce (available in the Asian aisle at most grocery stores) adds a deep flavor that's not at all "fishy"

1	(2 lb) unseasoned pork tenderloin
½ Tbsp	garlic, minced or pressed (about 1 clove)
2 Tbsp	fresh ginger, minced (or 1 tsp ground)
1 Tbsp	fish sauce
1 Tbsp	lite soy sauce
½ Tbsp	granulated sugar
1 Tbsp	sesame oil (optional)

1. Preheat grill or oven broiler (with rack 3 inches from heat source) on high temperature.
2. Remove visible fat from tenderloin and discard. Set tenderloin aside.
3. Combine garlic, ginger, fish sauce, soy sauce, sugar, and sesame oil (optional) in a small dish. Stir marinade until sugar dissolves.
4. Brush tenderloin with marinade or pour one-third of the marinade evenly over the pork. Place in oven or grill with lid closed.
5. Every 5 minutes, turn over the tenderloin and add 1 tablespoon of additional marinade, until meat is fully cooked (to a minimum internal temperature of 160 °F).
6. Let stand for 5 minutes.
7. Cut 12 slices, each about 1 inch thick. Serve three slices (about 3 oz cooked weight) per serving.

Tip: Delicious with steamed spinach and rice or Asian-style noodles (soba or udon).

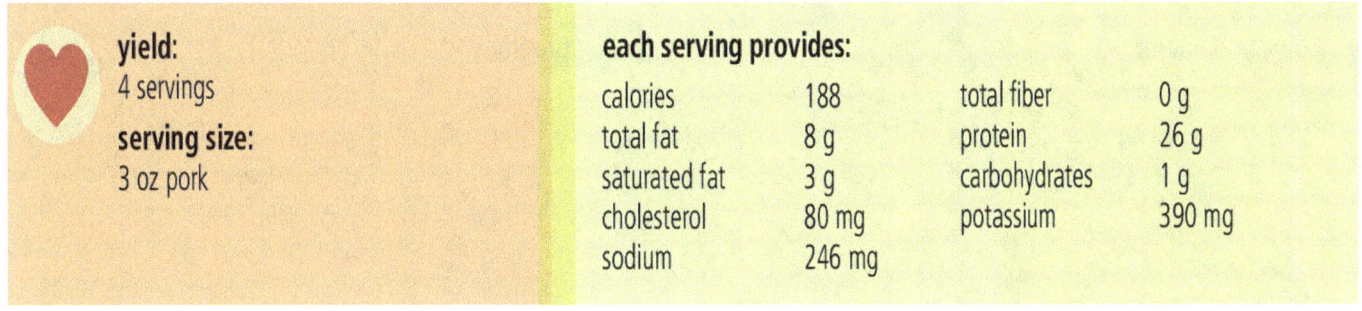

yield: 4 servings
serving size: 3 oz pork

each serving provides:

calories	188	total fiber	0 g
total fat	8 g	protein	26 g
saturated fat	3 g	carbohydrates	1 g
cholesterol	80 mg	potassium	390 mg
sodium	246 mg		

cold fusilli pasta with summer vegetables

Prep time: 20 minutes
Cook time: 10 minutes

a whole new twist on pasta salad!

8 oz	whole-wheat fusilli (spiral) pasta
2 C	cherry tomatoes, rinsed and halved
1	large green bell pepper, rinsed and sliced in pieces ¼ inch wide by 2 inches long
½ C	red onion, thinly sliced
1	medium zucchini, rinsed and shredded finely or sliced into small chunks (about 1 C)
1 can	(15½ oz) low-sodium chickpeas (or garbanzo beans), drained and rinsed
1 Tbsp	fresh basil, rinsed, dried, and cut into thin strips (or 1 tsp dried)
¼ tsp	salt
⅛ tsp	ground black pepper
1 Tbsp	extra virgin olive oil
2 Tbsp	balsamic vinegar
½ C	shredded parmesan cheese

1. In a 4-quart saucepan, bring 3 quarts of water to a boil over high heat.
2. Add pasta, and cook according to package directions for the shortest recommended time, about 8–9 minutes. Drain. Rinse pasta under cold running water to cool, about 3 minutes.
3. Place all the vegetables and beans in a large salad serving bowl. Season with basil, salt, and pepper.
4. Add the cooled pasta.
5. Combine olive oil and vinegar in a small bowl. Mix until completely blended. Pour over vegetables and pasta. Mix gently until well coated.
6. Divide into four equal portions. Top each with 2 tablespoons shredded parmesan cheese.

Note: If you can't find beans labeled "low-sodium," compare the Nutrition Facts panels to find the beans with the lowest amount of sodium. Rinsing can help further reduce the sodium level.

yield: 4 servings

serving size: about 1½ C pasta

each serving provides:

calories	418	total fiber	13 g
total fat	11 g	protein	21 g
saturated fat	3 g	carbohydrates	63 g
cholesterol:	10 mg	potassium	576 mg
sodium	455 mg		

deliciously healthy dinners

mushroom penne

Prep time: 15 minutes
Cook time: 15 minutes

a mushroom lover's dish that makes a quick and cozy meal at home or an elegant dish for company

8 oz	whole-wheat penne pasta
2 Tbsp	olive oil
8 oz	white mushrooms, rinsed and sliced
½ C	onion, thinly sliced
1 Tbsp	garlic, minced or pressed (about 2–3 cloves)
6 Tbsp	dry red wine
1 C	low-sodium chicken broth
¼ tsp	salt
¼ tsp	ground black pepper
1 tsp	dried thyme
4 Tbsp	shredded parmesan cheese

1. In a 4-quart saucepan, bring 3 quarts of water to a boil over high heat.
2. Add pasta, and cook according to package directions for the shortest recommended time, about 8 minutes.
3. While water heats and pasta cooks, warm olive oil in a large nonstick pan over medium heat.
4. Chop the mushrooms into bite-sized pieces. Cook the mushrooms in the oil for 5 minutes.
5. Meanwhile, slice onion and mince garlic. Add to mushrooms. Cook for 3 minutes, stirring occasionally.
6. Add wine. Cook and stir to loosen any flavorful browned bits to mix into the sauce. Stir in chicken broth, salt, pepper, and thyme.
7. Drain pasta. Stir into mushroom mixture. Continue simmering mixture until all moisture is absorbed, about 3 minutes.
8. Divide into four equal portions (each about 1¼ cups). Top each with 1 tablespoon shredded parmesan cheese.

Tip: Pairs beautifully with a fresh green salad.

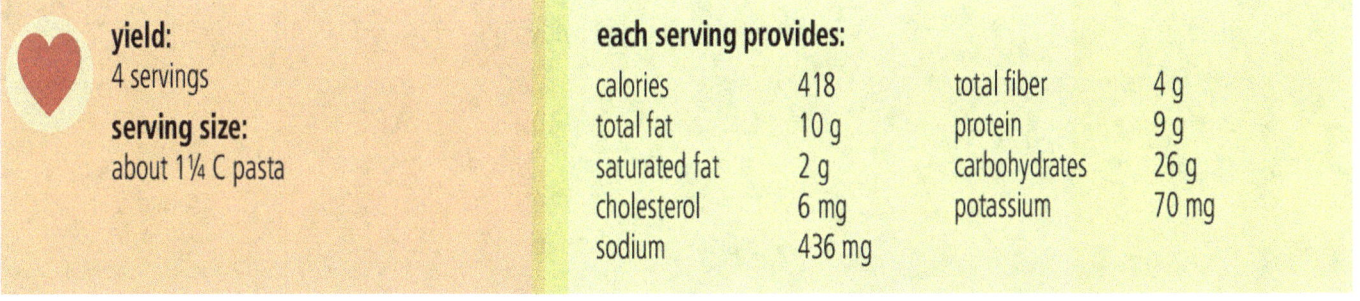

yield: 4 servings
serving size: about 1¼ C pasta

each serving provides:

calories	418	total fiber	4 g
total fat	10 g	protein	9 g
saturated fat	2 g	carbohydrates	26 g
cholesterol	6 mg	potassium	70 mg
sodium	436 mg		

rotini with spicy red pepper and almond sauce

Prep time: 15 minutes
Cook time: 15 minutes

spicy and crunchy pair together nicely to create this dish's unique sauce

8 oz	whole-wheat rotini (spiral) pasta
½ C	whole natural almonds, unsalted
1 jar	(12 oz) roasted red peppers
1 Tbsp	garlic, roughly chopped (about 2–3 cloves)
⅛ tsp	ground cayenne pepper
1 tsp	paprika
1 Tbsp	dried basil or parsley
1 tsp	red wine vinegar
½ tsp	salt
Ground black pepper to taste	

1. In a 4-quart saucepan, bring 3 quarts of water to a boil over high heat.
2. Add pasta, and cook according to package directions for the shortest recommended time, about 10 minutes. Drain pasta.
3. While the pasta cooks, toast almonds in a toaster oven or regular oven at 350 °F until lightly toasted, about 5–8 minutes. Set aside to cool.
4. Meanwhile, in a food processor or blender, add roasted red peppers and liquid, garlic, cayenne pepper, paprika, basil, vinegar, salt, and pepper. Blend until smooth, 1–2 minutes.
5. Add cooled almonds to the sauce in the processor. Pulse until the almonds are chunky.
6. After draining the pasta, return to pot. Add almond sauce. Toss until pasta is well coated.
7. Divide into four equal portions (about 2 cups).

Tip: Try adding chicken or seafood—or, for a vegetarian meal, just add cooked lima beans or edamame (green soybeans).

yield: 4 servings
serving size: 2 C pasta

each serving provides:

calories	322	total fiber	9 g
total fat	10 g	protein	12 g
saturated fat	1 g	carbohydrates	49 g
cholesterol	0 mg	potassium	47 mg
sodium	383 mg		

deliciously healthy dinners

pasta caprese

Prep time: 15 minutes
Cook time: 6 minutes

use the ripest tomatoes to create a fresh pasta sauce for this dish

8 oz	whole-wheat thin spaghetti
1 Tbsp	olive oil
4	large tomatoes, rinsed, cored, and cubed
¼ C	fresh basil leaves, rinsed, dried, and cut into ⅛-inch wide slivers
3 oz	part-skim mozzarella cheese (chunk package), cubed
8	pitted black olives, cut into long slivers

1. In a 4-quart saucepan, bring 3 quarts of water to a boil over high heat.

2. Add spaghetti, and cook according to package directions for the shortest recommended time, about 6 minutes. (Whole-wheat pasta tends to fall apart if overcooked.)

3. Reserve 1 cup of the cooking water, and set aside. Drain spaghetti.

4. Add the spaghetti back into the pasta pot. Toss with olive oil and just enough reserved water to coat well.

5. Add the tomatoes, basil, mozzarella, and olives. Toss gently until well mixed.

6. Divide pasta evenly among four dinner plates (about 2¼ cups each). Serve immediately.

Tip: Try serving with a fresh green salad drizzled with light vinaigrette dressing.

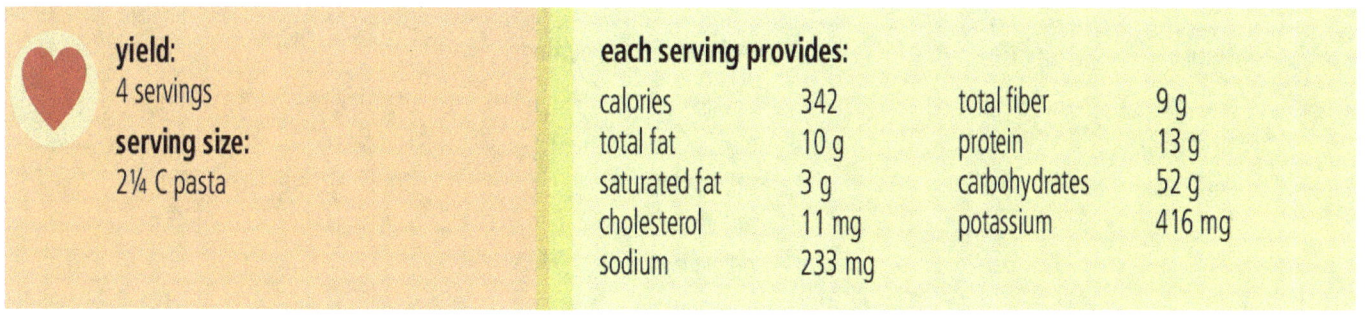

yield: 4 servings
serving size: 2¼ C pasta

each serving provides:

calories	342	total fiber	9 g
total fat	10 g	protein	13 g
saturated fat	3 g	carbohydrates	52 g
cholesterol	11 mg	potassium	416 mg
sodium	233 mg		

deliciously healthy dinners

linguini with clam sauce

Prep time: 20 minutes
Cook time: 20 minutes

a simple, yet timeless classic

12 oz	whole-wheat linguini
1 Tbsp	olive oil
1 Tbsp	garlic, minced (about 2–3 cloves)
1 Tbsp	lemon juice
1 C	low-sodium chicken broth
2 C	canned whole clams, undrained
2 Tbsp	fresh parsley, minced (or 2 tsp dried)
¼ tsp	salt
¼ tsp	ground black pepper
1 Tbsp	butter

1. In a 4-quart saucepan, bring 3 quarts of water to a boil over high heat.
2. Add linguini, and cook according to package directions for the shortest recommended time, about 9 minutes.
3. Heat olive oil in a large saucepan. Add garlic, and cook gently until it begins to soften, about 30 seconds. Do not brown.
4. Add lemon juice and chicken broth. Bring to a boil.
5. Add clams, along with liquid, parsley, salt, pepper, and butter. Simmer just until heated through, about 1–2 minutes. Do not overcook.
6. Strain the linguini, then add the pasta to the saucepan with the clams and mix well.
7. Divide into four equal portions (each about 2½ cups), and serve.

Tip: Lovely served with **Grilled Romaine Lettuce With Caesar Dressing** (on page 105).

yield: 4 servings

serving size: 2½ C pasta

each serving provides:

calories	476	total fiber	11 g
total fat	9 g	protein	34 g
saturated fat	3 g	carbohydrates	66 g
cholesterol	61 mg	potassium	681 mg
sodium	262 mg		

heavenly chicken with angel hair pasta

Prep time: 15 minutes
Cook time: 15 minutes

a mildly spicy sauce complements this simple, but heavenly, chicken and pasta dish

1 C	onion, finely chopped
1 Tbsp	garlic, minced or pressed (about 2–3 cloves)
4 C	broccoli florets, rinsed (about 1 lb)
1 Tbsp	olive oil
8 oz	very thinly sliced chicken breast, cut into ½-inch strips
1 jar	(26 oz) no-salt-added pasta sauce
¼ tsp	ground cayenne pepper
½ tsp	salt
8 oz	whole-wheat angel hair pasta
Cooking spray	

1. In a 4-quart saucepan, bring 3 quarts of water to a boil over high heat.

2. While the water heats, chop onion, mince garlic, and cut broccoli into tiny florets. Set aside.

3. In a large nonstick pan, heat olive oil until very hot. Add the chicken. Cook and stir until lightly browned on both sides, about 5–8 minutes. Place chicken on a clean plate, and cover to keep warm.

4. Coat pan with cooking spray. Over medium heat, cook and stir the onion for about 3 minutes. Add the garlic and broccoli. Cook and stir for 2 more minutes.

5. Return the chicken to the pan. Add entire jar of pasta sauce, cayenne pepper, and salt. Gently mix to blend ingredients. Cover. Simmer until chicken and vegetables are warmed through, about 4 minutes.

6. Drop pasta into boiling water. Cook according to package directions for the shortest recommended time, about 2 minutes. Drain.

7. Divide pasta among four dinner plates (about 1 cup each). Top each with one-fourth of the chicken and sauce mixture. Serve immediately.

yield:
4 servings

serving size:
about 2 C pasta and chicken

each serving provides:

calories	452	total fiber	13 g
total fat	10 g	protein	31 g
saturated fat	1 g	carbohydrates	66 g
cholesterol	48 mg	potassium	569 mg
sodium	412 mg		

whole-wheat bow tie pasta with puttanesca sauce

Prep time: 10 minutes
Cook time: 12 minutes

capers, olives, and anchovy paste will make this quick, but rich, sauce a weeknight favorite

8 oz	whole-wheat bow tie pasta (farfalle)
2 Tbsp	olive oil
1½ C	onion, diced
2 Tbsp	garlic, minced or pressed (about 5 cloves)
¼ tsp	cayenne pepper
2 tsp	anchovy paste (optional)
1 can	(35 oz) no-salt-added whole peeled tomatoes, coarsely chopped
1 Tbsp	capers
8	pitted black olives, each sliced lengthwise into 6 pieces
4	fresh parsley sprigs, rinsed and dried (optional)

1. In a 4-quart saucepan, bring 3 quarts of water to a boil over high heat.
2. Add pasta, and cook according to package directions for the shortest recommended time, about 10 minutes. Drain.
3. Meanwhile, in a large nonstick pan, heat olive oil over medium heat. Add onion. Cook and stir for 5 minutes, until onion begins to soften.
4. Add garlic, cayenne pepper, and anchovy paste. Cook and stir another 5 minutes.
5. Add chopped tomatoes, capers, and olives. Cook and stir until heated through.
6. Divide pasta among four dinner plates (about 1½ cups each). Spoon sauce over pasta. Garnish with parsley if desired.

Tip: Excellent with **Grilled Romaine Lettuce With Caesar Dressing** (on page 105) and pan-grilled shrimp or chicken.

yield: 4 servings

serving size: about 1½ C pasta

each serving provides:

calories	342	total fiber	12 g
total fat	8 g	protein	11 g
saturated fat	1 g	carbohydrates	62 g
cholesterol	9 mg	potassium	537 mg
sodium	455 mg		

deliciously healthy dinners

turkey bolognese with shell pasta

Prep time: 5 minutes
Cook time: 35 minutes

anise seed makes turkey taste like Italian sausage, with none of the saturated fat; the red wine and dried mushrooms make this a uniquely delicious dish

1½ C	dry red wine (optional)
½ oz	dried porcini mushrooms (optional)
1 C	onion, chopped
½ C	celery, rinsed and chopped
1 C	carrots, rinsed and thinly sliced or shredded
1 Tbsp	garlic, pressed or finely chopped (about 2–3 cloves)
1 Tbsp	olive oil
12 oz	99 percent lean ground turkey
1 tsp	anise seed
¼ tsp	salt
8 oz	medium shell pasta
4 Tbsp	no-salt-added tomato paste
½ C	shredded parmesan cheese

1. Optional step: Bring the wine to a boil in a medium saucepan. Break up the mushrooms, then stir them into the wine. Cover, reduce heat, and simmer for 20 minutes.

2. Finely chop the onion, celery, carrots, and garlic. Or you can coarsely chop them, place them in a food processor, and pulse until all vegetables are finely chopped.

3. In a 4-quart saucepan, bring 3 quarts of water to a boil over high heat.

4. While the water is heating up, warm the olive oil in a large nonstick pan over medium-high heat. Crumble in the ground turkey. Sprinkle with anise seed and salt. Cook for 5–10 minutes to brown, stirring occasionally.

5. Meanwhile, when the water comes to a boil, add pasta to boiling water. Cook according to package directions for the shortest recommended time, about 10–12 minutes.

6. Add vegetables to cooking turkey. Reduce heat to medium. Cook and stir 10 minutes until all vegetables are soft, but not browned. Add tomato paste, and simmer for an additional 5–10 minutes. (Continue to optional step 7 if including the optional ingredients; otherwise, skip to step 8.)

continued on page 75

turkey bolognese with shell pasta (continued)

7. Optional step: While the pasta and turkey mixture cooks, strain mushrooms, draining unabsorbed wine directly into the turkey mixture. Place mushrooms on a cutting board and chop finely, or place in food processor and pulse once or twice to more finely chop mushrooms. Stir mushrooms into turkey mixture. Simmer for 10–15 minutes to blend flavors.

8. Drain pasta. Add pasta to turkey mixture (the minimum internal temperature of cooked turkey should be 165 °F). Stir to blend well.

9. Divide pasta mixture evenly (about 2 cups each) among four dinner plates. Top each with 2 tablespoons of shredded parmesan cheese.

Tip: Serve with a side of sliced fresh tomatoes, cucumbers, and balsamic vinegar.

yield: 4 servings

serving size: about 2 C pasta

each serving provides:

calories	463	total fiber	5 g
total fat	9 g	protein	35 g
saturated fat	3 g	carbohydrates	47 g
cholesterol	63 mg	potassium	734 mg
sodium	465 mg		

lemon and garlic pasta with pan-seared scallops

Prep time: 10 minutes
Cook time: 10 minutes

for a delicious and quick meal, this pasta and scallops dish will hit the spot

1	large lemon, grated for zest (and freshly squeezed for 2 Tbsp lemon juice)
1 Tbsp	garlic, minced or pressed (about 2–3 cloves)
2 Tbsp	olive oil, divided into two 1-Tbsp portions
16	large sea scallops (about 1 lb)
¼ tsp	salt
⅛ tsp	ground black pepper
8 oz	very thin spaghetti (vermicelli or angel hair)
2 Tbsp	shredded parmesan cheese

1. In a 4-quart saucepan, bring 3 quarts of water to a boil over high heat. When the water boils, reduce heat to simmer until you're ready to cook the pasta (step 5).

2. While the water is heating up, use a grater to take off small peels of the skin of the lemon into a small saucepan. Cut the lemon in half and squeeze the juice into the pan and remove pits. Use the back of a large spoon to press the inside of the lemon to extract more juice. Add the garlic and 1 tablespoon of the olive oil to the saucepan. Stir to blend well. Place on stovetop on low heat.

continued on page 77

76 deliciously healthy dinners

lemon and garlic pasta with pan-seared scallops (continued)

3. Heat a large nonstick pan or grill pan on high temperature until very hot. Sprinkle the scallops with salt, pepper, and 1 tablespoon of olive oil. Toss to coat well.

4. Place the scallops in the hot pan. Cook about 4 minutes on each side, or until scallops are well browned and firm and milky white to the center (to a minimum internal temperature of 145 °F).

5. After turning the scallops to the second side, drop the pasta into the boiling water. Set temperature on medium, and cook for 2 minutes or the shortest recommended time according to package directions.

6. When the pasta is done, set aside ½ cup of the cooking water. Drain the pasta. Return drained pasta to the pot, and toss with the warm olive oil mixture and the ½ cup reserved pasta water.

7. Divide the pasta equally among four plates (about 1 cup per plate). Top each with four scallops.

8. Garnish each dish with ½ tablespoon of shredded parmesan cheese. Serve immediately.

Tip: Delicious with a side of **Baby Spinach With Golden Raisins and Pine Nuts** (on page 107).

yield: 4 servings

serving size: 4 scallops, 1 C pasta

each serving provides:

calories	376	total fiber	2 g
total fat	9 g	protein	28 g
saturated fat	2 g	carbohydrates	43 g
cholesterol	48 mg	potassium	426 mg
sodium	429 mg		

deliciously healthy dinners

classic macaroni and cheese

Prep time: 5 minutes
Cook time: 40 minutes

this recipe proves you don't have to give up your favorite dishes to eat heart healthy meals—here's a lower fat version of a true classic

2 C	macaroni
½ C	onion, chopped
½ C	fat-free evaporated milk
1	medium egg, lightly beaten
¼ tsp	ground black pepper
1¼ C	(4 oz) low-fat sharp cheddar cheese, finely shredded
Cooking spray	

1. Cook macaroni according to package directions—but do not add salt to the cooking water. Drain and set aside.
2. Spray a casserole dish with nonstick cooking spray.
3. Preheat oven to 350 °F.
4. Lightly spray a saucepan with nonstick cooking spray. Add onion to saucepan and sauté for about 3 minutes over medium heat.
5. In a bowl, combine macaroni, onion, and the remaining ingredients, and mix thoroughly.
6. Transfer mixture into casserole dish.
7. Bake for 25 minutes or until bubbly. Let stand for 10 minutes before serving.

Tip: Pairs nicely with steamed broccoli and garlic.

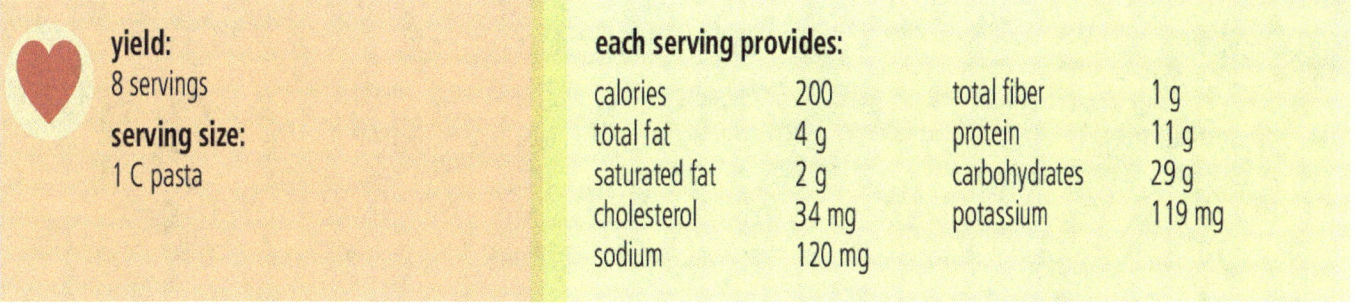

yield: 8 servings

serving size: 1 C pasta

each serving provides:

calories	200	total fiber	1 g
total fat	4 g	protein	11 g
saturated fat	2 g	carbohydrates	29 g
cholesterol	34 mg	potassium	119 mg
sodium	120 mg		

deliciously healthy dinners

sweet and sour seashells

Prep time: 5 minutes
Cook time: 10 minutes

drain the marinade before serving this dish to lower the fat and sodium—but keep all the great taste

1 lb	small seashell pasta (9 C cooked)
2 Tbsp	vegetable oil
¾ C	sugar
½ C	cider vinegar
½ C	wine vinegar
½ C	water
3 Tbsp	prepared mustard
⅛ tsp	ground black pepper
1 jar	(2 oz) sliced pimientos
2	small cucumbers, rinsed
2	small onions, thinly sliced
18	leaves lettuce, rinsed and dried

1. Cook pasta according to package directions—but do not add salt to the cooking water. Drain, rinse with cold water, and drain again. Stir in oil.

2. Transfer to a 4-quart bowl. In blender, place sugar, vinegars, water, prepared mustard, pepper, and pimientos. Process at low speed for 15–20 seconds, or just enough so flecks of pimiento can be seen. Pour over pasta.

3. Score cucumber peels with fork tines (optional). Cut cucumbers in half lengthwise, then slice thinly. Add to pasta, along with onions. Toss well.

4. Drain, and serve; each serving size is 1 cup pasta on two lettuce leaves.

Tip: Pairs nicely with grilled chicken or shrimp.

yield: 9 servings

serving size: 1 C pasta, 2 lettuce leaves

each serving provides:

calories	316	total fiber	4 g
total fat	4 g	protein	8 g
saturated fat	0 g	carbohydrates	62 g
cholesterol	0 mg	potassium	300 mg
sodium	70 mg		

deliciously healthy dinners

tuscan beans with tomatoes and oregano

Prep time: 15 minutes
Cook time: 0 minutes

dine outside on a warm summer evening with this cool and satisfying salad

1 can	(15½ oz) low-sodium chickpeas (or garbanzo beans), drained and rinsed
2 C	cherry tomatoes, rinsed and halved
1 Tbsp	olive oil
1 tsp	balsamic vinegar
2 Tbsp	fresh oregano, minced (or 1 tsp dried)
⅛ tsp	ground black pepper
½ tsp	salt-free seasoning blend
4	whole inner leaves of romaine lettuce, rinsed and dried

1. In a large salad bowl, combine beans and tomatoes.
2. In a small bowl, combine olive oil, vinegar, oregano, pepper, and salt-free seasoning blend. Using a wire whisk, beat the ingredients until they blend into one thick sauce at the point where the oil and vinegar no longer separate.
3. Pour the dressing over the beans and tomatoes, and mix gently to coat.
4. Line four salad bowls with one romaine lettuce leaf each.
5. Top each leaf with one-fourth of the bean mixture, and serve.

main dishes — **vegetarian**

Tip: Serve with a fresh green salad and crusty bread to soak up the delicious dressing.
Note: If you can't find beans labeled "low-sodium," compare the Nutrition Facts panels to find the beans with the lowest amount of sodium. Rinsing can help further reduce the sodium level.

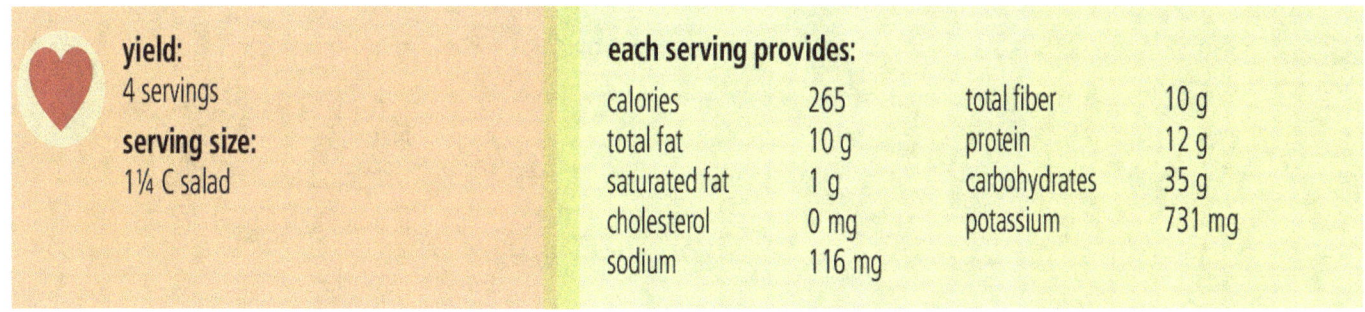

yield:
4 servings

serving size:
1¼ C salad

each serving provides:

calories	265	total fiber	10 g
total fat	10 g	protein	12 g
saturated fat	1 g	carbohydrates	35 g
cholesterol	0 mg	potassium	731 mg
sodium	116 mg		

deliciously healthy dinners

caribbean casserole

Prep time: 10 minutes
Cook time: 10 minutes

this tropical-inspired dish is gently spiced for a rich flavor

1	medium onion, chopped
½	green bell pepper, rinsed and diced
1 Tbsp	canola oil
1 can	(14½ oz) stewed tomatoes
1 can	(15½ oz) low-sodium black beans (or beans of your choice), drained and rinsed
1 tsp	dried oregano
½ tsp	garlic powder
1½ C	instant brown rice, uncooked

1. Sauté onion and green pepper in canola oil, in a large pan, until tender. Do not brown.
2. Add tomatoes and beans (including liquid from both), as well as oregano and garlic powder. Bring to a boil.
3. Stir in rice and cover. Reduce heat to simmer for 5 minutes. Remove from heat, and let stand for 5 minutes before serving.

Tip: Finish the meal with delicious tropical fruit, such as mangoes, papayas, or pineapple.

Note: If you can't find beans labeled "low-sodium," compare the Nutrition Facts panels to find the beans with the lowest amount of sodium. Rinsing can help further reduce the sodium level.

yield:
10 servings

serving size:
1 C casserole

each serving provides:

calories	185	total fiber	7 g
total fat	1 g	protein	7 g
saturated fat	0 g	carbohydrates	37 g
cholesterol	0 mg	potassium	292 mg
sodium	297 mg		

deliciously healthy dinners

red beans and rice

Prep time: 5 minutes
Cook time: 25 minutes

this quick and easy classic Cajun dish is great for a weeknight meal at home, or fun to serve at a party

1 Tbsp	olive oil
1 C	onion, cut into ½-inch pieces
1 C	green bell pepper, rinsed and diced
1 Tbsp	garlic, minced or pressed (about 2–3 cloves)
1½ tsp	ground cumin
1½ tsp	dried oregano
1 can	(14½ oz) low-sodium chicken broth or vegetable broth
½ C	instant brown rice, uncooked
2 cans	(15 oz each) low-sodium red kidney beans, drained and rinsed

1. Heat oil in a 12-inch sauté pan over medium heat. Cook onion, stirring occasionally, for 5 minutes, until pieces begin to soften, but not brown.

2. Meanwhile, dice green pepper into pieces about ¼ inch in size. Tip: Slice pepper lengthwise into ¼-inch strips. Holding the strips together, cut crosswise into ¼-inch pieces. Add green pepper to cooking onion. Cover. Cook for 5 minutes, stirring occasionally.

3. While the green pepper and onion cook, mince the garlic. Add garlic, cumin, and oregano to the sauté pan. Cook and stir for 1 minute.

4. Add broth and rice to the sauté pan with green pepper and onion. Stir well, cover, and simmer for 10 minutes.

5. Meanwhile, drain beans and rinse thoroughly.

6. Add beans to sauté pan. Stir well. Cover. Simmer for 5 minutes to heat beans and blend flavors.

main dishes · vegetarian

Tip: Try serving with steamed broccoli on the side.
Note: If you can't find beans labeled "low-sodium," compare the Nutrition Facts panels to find the beans with the lowest amount of sodium. Rinsing can help further reduce the sodium level.

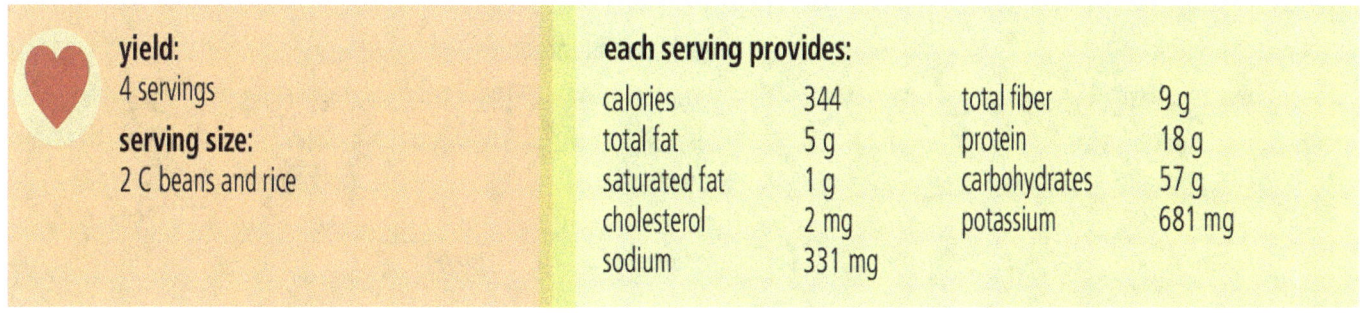

yield: 4 servings
serving size: 2 C beans and rice

each serving provides:

calories	344	total fiber	9 g
total fat	5 g	protein	18 g
saturated fat	1 g	carbohydrates	57 g
cholesterol	2 mg	potassium	681 mg
sodium	331 mg		

corn and black bean burritos

Prep time: 20 minutes
Cook time: 5 minutes

these burritos are high in flavor and easy to make

¼ C	scallions (green onions), rinsed and sliced into ¼-inch wide circles, including green tops
¼ C	celery, rinsed and finely diced
1¼ C	frozen yellow corn
½	ripe avocado, peeled and diced
2 Tbsp	fresh cilantro, chopped (or substitute 2 tsp dried coriander)
1 can	(15½ oz) black beans, drained and rinsed
¼ C	reduced-fat shredded cheddar cheese
¼ C	salsa or taco sauce (look for lowest sodium version)
12	(9-inch) whole-wheat tortillas

1. Preheat oven to 350 °F.
2. Combine scallions, celery, and corn in a small saucepan. Add just enough water to cover.
3. Cover, bring to a boil, and reduce heat to medium. Simmer for 5 minutes, until vegetables soften. Drain vegetables. Set aside to cool.
4. Combine avocado, cilantro, and beans in a large mixing bowl. Add cheese and salsa, and mix.
5. When corn mixture has cooled slightly, add to avocado mixture.
6. In a large nonstick pan over medium heat, warm each tortilla for about 15 seconds on each side. Place each tortilla on a flat surface. Spoon ⅓ cup of the mixture into the center of the tortilla. Fold the top and bottom of the tortilla over the filling. Fold in the sides to make a closed packet.
7. Repeat with the remaining tortillas.
8. When all tortillas are wrapped, continue heating in the oven 5 minutes, until all are warm and cheese is melted.

Tip: Try serving with extra salsa on the side.

yield: 12 servings
serving size: 1 burrito

each serving provides:

calories	189	total fiber	3 g
total fat	3 g	protein	8 g
saturated fat	0 g	carbohydrates	34 g
cholesterol	0 mg	potassium	204 mg
sodium	257 mg		

lentils with brown rice and kale

Prep time: 5 minutes
Cook time: 35 minutes

for a different flavor and even more fiber and protein, try quinoa in place of the brown rice; quinoa (pronounced KEEN-wah) is a grain native to South America

For lentils and kale:

1 C	brown lentils, rinsed
¼ tsp	salt
⅛ tsp	ground black pepper
4 C	kale, with heavy stems removed, rinsed and dried

For brown rice:

1 C	instant brown rice, uncooked (for quinoa, follow cooking instructions on box)
¼ tsp	salt
½ tsp	dried basil

For onion:

2 Tbsp	olive oil
2 C	onion, diced
¼ tsp	salt
⅛ tsp	ground black pepper

1. Rinse lentils thoroughly in a fine wire colander, and remove any stones or debris.

2. In a 4-quart saucepan, cover lentils with 2½ cups of water. Add salt and pepper. Cover, and bring to a boil over high heat. Reduce heat. Simmer for 15 minutes (until adding kale in step 5).

3. In another saucepan, bring 2 cups of water to a boil. Add rice, salt, and basil. Cover, and cook for 10 minutes. Set aside.

4. In a medium sauté pan, warm olive oil over medium heat and add onion, salt, and pepper. Cook and stir until the onion pieces become soft and dark brown (caramelized), but not burnt. If the onions start to stick to the pan, add a few drops of water and scrape the onions loose. Keep cooking until onions are completely caramelized (about 10–15 minutes total). Remove from pan and set aside.

5. After the lentils have cooked for 15 minutes, lightly place the kale on top of the lentils. Do not stir. Cover. The kale will steam while the lentils continue to cook, for another 15 minutes.

continued on page 89

deliciously healthy dinners

lentils with brown rice and kale (continued)

6. When the lentils are tender, but not mushy, mix the lentils, kale, and caramelized onions in the sauté pan and stir.

7. To serve, put 1 cup of the lentil mixture, in the form of a ring, on each of four dinner plates. Fill the center of each ring with one-fourth of the brown rice. Serve immediately.

Tip: For starters, try the **Creamy Squash Soup With Shredded Apples** (on page 114).

yield:
4 servings

serving size:
1 C lentils, ⅓ C rice, ½ C kale

each serving provides:

calories	456	total fiber	19 g
total fat	9 g	protein	21 g
saturated fat	1 g	carbohydrates	77 g
cholesterol	0 mg	potassium	864 mg
sodium	472 mg		

deliciously healthy dinners

broccoli with asian tofu

Prep time: 20 minutes
Cook time: 20 minutes

the wonder of tofu is that it takes on the flavor of your favorite marinade

1 pkg	(16 oz) firm tofu, drained
2 Tbsp	lite soy sauce
1 tsp	sesame oil (optional)
½ Tbsp	brown sugar
1 Tbsp	fresh ginger root, finely chopped or shredded (or 1 tsp ground)
1 lb	fresh broccoli, rinsed and cut into individual spears
1 Tbsp	peanut oil or vegetable oil
¼ tsp	crushed red pepper
4 Tbsp	garlic, peeled and thinly sliced (about 8 cloves)
1 Tbsp	sesame seeds (optional)
Cooking spray	

1. Slice tofu into eight pieces. Place on a plate or flat surface covered with three paper towels. Top with four more paper towels. Top with another flat plate or cutting board. Press down evenly and gently to squeeze out moisture. Throw away paper towels. Replace with fresh paper towels and press again. (The more liquid you remove, the more sauce the tofu will absorb.)

2. Place tofu in a bowl just big enough to hold all eight pieces lying on their widest side without overlapping.

3. In a small bowl, combine the soy sauce, sesame oil, brown sugar, and ginger into a marinade, and stir thoroughly. Pour over tofu. Carefully turn the tofu several times to coat well. Set aside.

continued on page 91

broccoli with asian tofu (continued)

4. Meanwhile, heat a large nonstick sauté pan coated with cooking spray. Add broccoli and sauté for about 5 minutes, until it turns bright green and becomes tender and crispy. Remove broccoli from pan and set aside.

5. Heat a grill pan or flat sauté pan over high heat. Drain tofu, reserving marinade. Place on grill pan to heat for about 3 minutes. Gently turn. Heat the second side for 3 minutes.

6. At the same time, in the sauté pan over medium-low heat, warm the peanut oil, crushed red pepper, and garlic until the garlic softens and begins to turn brown, about 30 seconds to 1 minute. Add broccoli and reserved marinade, and gently mix until well-coated.

7. Place two slices of tofu on each plate with one-quarter of the broccoli and marinade mixture. Sprinkle with sesame seeds (optional).

Tip: Delicious served on top of brown rice or Asian-style noodles (soba or udon).

yield: 4 servings

serving size: 2 slices tofu, with broccoli and marinade mixture

each serving provides:

calories	183	total fiber	4 g
total fat	11 g	protein	14 g
saturated fat	2 g	carbohydrates	13 g
cholesterol	0 mg	potassium	556 mg
sodium	341 mg		

three-bean chili with chunky tomatoes

spice is nice, especially on a chilly night!

Prep time: 10 minutes
Cook time: 20 minutes

2 Tbsp	canola oil
1 C	onion, coarsely chopped
½ C	celery, rinsed and chopped
1 C	green bell pepper, rinsed and diced
1 can	(15½ oz) low-sodium black beans, drained and rinsed
1 can	(15½ oz) low-sodium red kidney beans, drained and rinsed
1 can	(15½ oz) low-sodium pinto beans, drained and rinsed
2 cans	(14½ oz each) no-salt-added diced tomatoes with basil, garlic, and oregano
1 Tbsp	ground cumin
1 Tbsp	chili powder

1. In an 8-quart soup or pasta pot, heat the oil over medium heat until hot but not smoking. Add onion. Cook and stir until onion starts to soften, about 5 minutes.
2. Add celery and green pepper. Cook and stir another 5 minutes, until all vegetables soften.
3. Add drained and rinsed beans to pot.
4. Stir in tomatoes, cumin, and chili powder.
5. Bring to a boil. Cover, reduce heat, and simmer 10–20 minutes to blend flavors.
6. Serve immediately.

Tip: Delicious with rice or a side of **Good-for-You Cornbread** (on page 119).

Note: If you can't find beans labeled "low-sodium," compare the Nutrition Facts panels to find the beans with the lowest amount of sodium. Rinsing can help further reduce the sodium level.

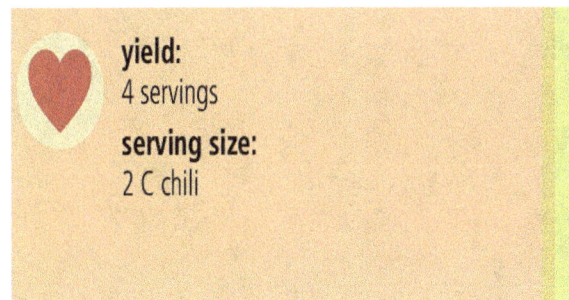

yield: 4 servings
serving size: 2 C chili

each serving provides:

calories	443	total fiber	16 g
total fat	8 g	protein	22 g
saturated fat	0 g	carbohydrates	73 g
cholesterol	0 mg	potassium	1,411 mg
sodium	331 mg		

caribbean pink beans

Prep time: Soak beans overnight; then 10 minutes
Cook time: 60 minutes

this dish stays healthy by using beans prepared without lard or other fat

1 lb	dried pink beans
2	medium plantains, finely chopped
1	large tomato, rinsed and finely chopped
1	small red bell pepper, rinsed and finely chopped
1	medium white onion, finely chopped
1½ Tbsp	garlic, minced (about 3 cloves)
1½ tsp	salt

1. Rinse and pick through beans for rocks and other debris (discard these). Put beans in large pot, and add 10 cups of water. Place pot in refrigerator, and allow beans to soak overnight.

2. Place the soaked and drained beans in a large pot with enough water to cover them by about 1 inch. Boil gently with lid tilted until beans are soft, about 1 hour. Add more water while beans are cooking if water level drops below the top of the beans.

3. Add plantains, tomato, red pepper, onion, garlic, and salt. Continue cooking at low heat until plantains are soft.

4. Serve warm.

Tip: Try serving with a whole grain, such as **Quinoa With Paprika and Cumin** (on page 118).

yield:
16 servings

serving size:
½ C beans

each serving provides:

calories	133	total fiber	5 g
total fat	0 g	protein	6 g
saturated fat	0 g	carbohydrates	28 g
cholesterol	0 mg	potassium	495 mg
sodium	205 mg		

deliciously healthy dinners

edamame stew

this spicy stew can be frozen for later use

Prep time: 20 minutes
Cook time: 20 minutes

1 bag	(16 oz) frozen shelled edamame (green soybeans)*
1 can	(35 oz) no-salt-added Italian whole peeled tomatoes with basil, diced into small chunks
2 C	zucchini, rinsed, quartered, and sliced
1 C	yellow onion, diced
1 Tbsp	olive oil
1 Tbsp	ground cumin
¼ tsp	ground cayenne pepper
½ tsp	ground allspice *(or substitute cinnamon or pumpkin pie spice)*
2 Tbsp	garlic, minced or pressed (about 5 cloves)
1 C	frozen yellow corn
¼ tsp	salt
2 Tbsp	lemon juice (or 1 large lemon, freshly juiced)
½ tsp	dried oregano

1. Place frozen edamame in a deep saucepan with just enough water to cover. Bring to a boil over high heat. Reduce heat to medium and cover. Cook for 5 minutes. Drain. Set aside.
2. While soybeans cook, chop tomatoes, zucchini, and onion.
3. In a large nonstick sauté pan, cook onion in olive oil over medium heat until soft, about 5 minutes.
4. Stir in cumin, cayenne pepper, and allspice (or cinnamon/pumpkin pie spice). Cook and stir for about 2 minutes.
5. Add garlic. Cook and stir for 1 minute.
6. Stir in the drained edamame, tomatoes, zucchini, corn, and salt.
7. Cover. Simmer until zucchini is tender, about 15 minutes.
8. Stir in lemon juice and oregano.
9. Serve immediately.

main dishes / vegetarian

Tip: Serve over brown rice for a complete meal.

* Frozen edamame is available in most grocery stores.

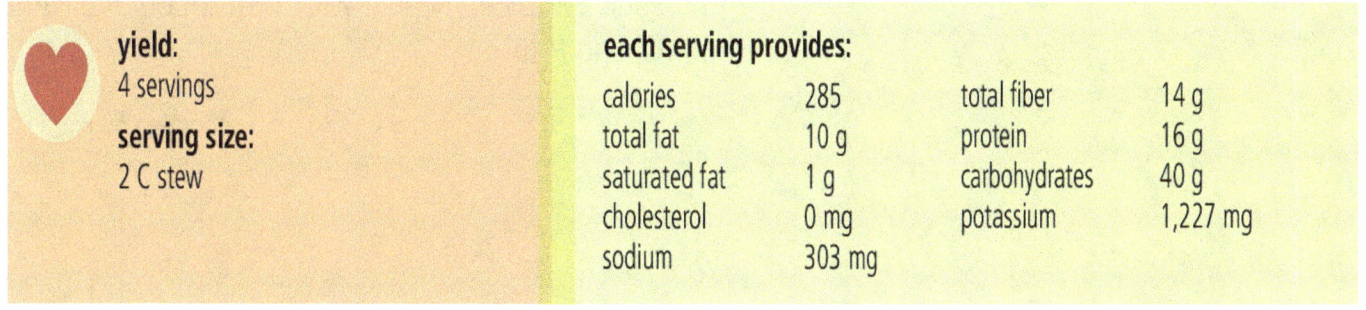

yield: 4 servings
serving size: 2 C stew

each serving provides:

calories	285	total fiber	14 g
total fat	10 g	protein	16 g
saturated fat	1 g	carbohydrates	40 g
cholesterol	0 mg	potassium	1,227 mg
sodium	303 mg		

deliciously healthy dinners

tofu stir-fry with spicy sauce

Prep time: 40 minutes
Cook time: 10 minutes

have all your ingredients cut and ready to go, because when the cooking starts, things happen really fast!

1 pkg	(16 oz) firm tofu, drained
¼ tsp	ground cayenne pepper
½ tsp	ground ginger or pumpkin pie spice (or try Chinese five-spice mix)
3 Tbsp	light teriyaki sauce
1 tsp	sesame oil (optional)
1 can	(14½ oz) low-sodium chicken broth or vegetable broth, divided
1 Tbsp	cornstarch
1 Tbsp	canola oil, divided into three 1-tsp portions
½ head	Chinese (napa) cabbage, rinsed and cut in ½-inch strips (6–8 C)
1 C	scallions (green onions), rinsed and sliced
1 Tbsp	garlic, minced or pressed (about 2–3 cloves)
1 C	carrots, peeled, thinly sliced or shredded
1 C	red bell pepper, rinsed and sliced
1 can	(8 oz) water chestnuts, sliced

1. Slice tofu lengthwise into four pieces. Place on a plate or flat surface covered with three paper towels. Cover with three more layers. Press evenly and gently with a flat plate or cutting board to squeeze out water. Throw away paper towels. Replace with fresh paper towels and press again. Restack the slices and cut into ½-inch wide strips. Place tofu in a bowl just big enough to hold all strips lying on their widest side without overlapping.

2. In a small bowl, combine cayenne pepper, ginger (or pumpkin pie spice/Chinese five-spice mix), teriyaki sauce, sesame oil (optional), and ½ cup of the chicken broth. Stir well, and then pour over the tofu. Set aside for 20 minutes.

3. Combine the remaining chicken broth and the cornstarch. Stir until cornstarch dissolves. Set aside.

4. In a large wok or large nonstick pan, heat 1 teaspoon of canola oil until very hot, but not smoking. While the pan heats, drain tofu marinade into cornstarch mixture.

5. Place half the tofu slices in the hot pan. Cook just until brown, about 1 minute per side. Remove from pan and set aside. Repeat with 1 teaspoon of oil and remaining tofu.

continued on page 97

tofu stir-fry with spicy sauce (continued)

6. Add the last teaspoon of oil to the pan. Stir in half the cabbage, beginning with the stalk end, the scallions, and the garlic. Cook and stir over high heat for 2 minutes.

7. Add the carrots, red pepper, and remaining cabbage. Cook and stir for 1 minute.

8. Add the water chestnuts and tofu. Cook and stir for 1 minute.

9. Stir the cornstarch mixture, then add to the pan. Reduce heat to medium. Cook and stir for 1 minute, until sauce thickens and all ingredients are well mixed and thoroughly coated with sauce. Serve immediately.

Tip: Delicious with steamed rice or Asian-style noodles (soba or udon).

yield: 4 servings

serving size: 2 C tofu and vegetables

each serving provides:

calories	232	total fiber	8 g
total fat	10 g	protein	16 g
saturated fat	1 g	carbohydrates	23 g
cholesterol	0 mg	potassium	1,504 mg
sodium	289 mg		

asparagus with lemon sauce

lemon sauce makes fresh asparagus the perfect side dish for fish, scallops, chicken, or meat dishes

Prep time: 5 minutes
Cook time: 10 minutes

20	medium asparagus spears, rinsed and trimmed
1	fresh lemon, rinsed (for peel and juice)
2 Tbsp	reduced-fat mayonnaise
1 Tbsp	dried parsley
⅛ tsp	ground black pepper
1/16 tsp	salt

1. Place 1 inch of water in a 4-quart pot with a lid. Place a steamer basket inside the pot, and add asparagus. Cover and bring to a boil over high heat. Reduce heat to medium. Cook for 5–10 minutes, until asparagus is easily pierced with a sharp knife. Do not overcook.

2. While the asparagus cooks, grate the lemon zest into a small bowl. Cut the lemon in half and squeeze the juice into the bowl. Use the back of a spoon to press out extra juice and remove pits. Add mayonnaise, parsley, pepper, and salt. Stir well. Set aside.

3. When the asparagus is tender, remove the pot from the heat. Place asparagus spears in a serving bowl. Drizzle the lemon sauce evenly over the asparagus (about 1½ teaspoons per portion) and serve.

yield: 4 servings

serving size: 5 spears, 1½ tsp sauce

each serving provides:

calories	39	total fiber	2 g
total fat	0 g	protein	2 g
saturated fat	0 g	carbohydrates	7 g
cholesterol	0 mg	potassium	241 mg
sodium	107 mg		

deliciously healthy dinners

cauliflower with whole-wheat breadcrumbs

Prep time: 10 minutes
Cook time: 10 minutes

this side dish is rich in flavor, but low in calories

1 slice	whole-wheat bread
1	medium cauliflower head, rinsed
¼ tsp	salt
1 Tbsp	soft tub margarine
⅛ tsp	ground black pepper

1. Place the bread in a toaster oven on very low heat. Toast as long as possible without burning (about 5 minutes).

2. While bread toasts, trim leaves and stalks from cauliflower. Cut into individual florets.

3. Place 1 inch of water in a 4-quart pot with lid. Insert steamer basket, and place cauliflower in basket. Sprinkle with salt. Cover. Bring to a boil over high heat. Reduce heat to medium. Steam for 5–8 minutes, until easily pierced with a sharp knife. Do not overcook.

4. While cauliflower steams, break toast into small pieces. Pulse toast in food processor until medium-sized crumbs form. Tip: If you don't have a food processor, break or crush the toasted bread into finer pieces or buy whole-wheat breadcrumbs and use 2 tablespoons.

5. When cauliflower is done, remove from heat. Melt margarine in another pan over medium heat. Add breadcrumbs and pepper. Cook and stir, about 5 minutes. Add cauliflower to pan with breadcrumbs. Toss until well coated. Serve immediately.

yield:
4 servings

serving size:
1 C cauliflower

each serving provides:

calories	45	total fiber	2 g
total fat	4 g	protein	2 g
saturated fat	0 g	carbohydrates	5 g
cholesterol	0 mg	potassium	152 mg
sodium	120 mg		

grilled romaine lettuce with caesar dressing

Prep time: 20 minutes
Cook time: 5 minutes

try this new approach to salad—grill it!

1 slice	whole-wheat bread
2	heads romaine lettuce, rinsed and halved lengthwise
4 tsp	olive oil
4 tsp	light Caesar dressing
4 Tbsp	shredded parmesan cheese
16	cherry tomatoes, rinsed and halved

1. Preheat grill pan on high temperature.
2. Cube the bread. Spread in a single layer on a foil-covered tray for a toaster oven or conventional oven. Toast to a medium-brown color and crunchy texture. Remove. Allow to cool.
3. Brush the cut side of each half of romaine lettuce with 1 teaspoon of olive oil.
4. Place cut side down on a grill pan on the stovetop. Cook just until grill marks appear and romaine is heated through, about 2–5 minutes.
5. Place each romaine half on a large salad plate. Top each with one-fourth of the bread cubes. Drizzle each with 1 teaspoon of light Caesar dressing. Sprinkle each with 1 tablespoon of shredded parmesan cheese. Garnish with eight tomato halves around each plate.

yield: 4 servings

serving size: ½ head of romaine lettuce with toppings

each serving provides:

calories	162	total fiber	8 g
total fat	8 g	protein	8 g
saturated fat	2 g	carbohydrates	17 g
cholesterol	6 mg	potassium	931 mg
sodium	241 mg		

baby spinach with
golden raisins and pine nuts

Prep time: 0 minutes
Cook time: 10 minutes

sweet golden raisins and crunchy pine nuts make this a fabulous way to get your spinach

4 Tbsp	pine nuts
2 bags	(10 oz each) leaf spinach, rinsed
⅔ C	golden seedless raisins
⅛ tsp	ground nutmeg
⅛ tsp	salt

1. In a medium nonstick pan over high heat, cook and stir the pine nuts until they begin to brown lightly and smell toasted, but not burnt. Set the pine nuts aside in another dish.

2. Return the pan to the burner over medium-high heat. Add ¼ cup water. As it begins to boil, add a small handful of the spinach. Cook and stir just until it begins to wilt. Then push it to the side of the pan, and add another ¼ cup water and handful of spinach. Continue until all the spinach has been cooked, adding the raisins with the last handful of spinach.

3. Sprinkle with nutmeg and salt. Cook and stir until all the spinach is wilted and the raisins are warm.

4. Remove from heat. Press out excess water. Place 1 cup spinach and raisins in a serving bowl. Top with pine nuts.

side dishes — **vegetable**

yield: 4 servings
serving size: 1 C spinach and raisins

each serving provides:

calories	76	total fiber	3 g
total fat	3 g	protein	3 g
saturated fat	0 g	carbohydrates	13 g
cholesterol	0 mg	potassium	510 mg
sodium	130 mg		

deliciously healthy dinners

roasted beets with orange sauce

this colorful side dish comes alive with orange flavor

Prep time: 10 minutes
Cook time: 45 minutes

1½ lb	small beets, leaves trimmed, peeled and cut into four chunks
1 tsp	olive oil
1	orange, rinsed (for peel and juice)
½ tsp	anise seeds (optional)

1. Preheat oven to 450 °F. Cover a baking sheet with aluminum foil for easy cleanup.
2. In a medium bowl, toss the beets with the olive oil until well coated.
3. Spread beets on baking sheet in a single layer.
4. Bake 30–40 minutes. When done, beets should be easily pierced with a sharp knife.
5. While beets bake, grate the zest from the orange. Place in a small bowl. Cut the orange in half. Squeeze the juice (about ½ cup) into the bowl with the orange zest. (Use a large spoon to press the inside of the orange to extract more juice.) Add anise seeds (optional). Set aside.
6. When the beets are tender, return them to the tossing bowl. Pour the juice mixture over the beets. Mix well to coat, and serve.

yield: 4 servings
serving size: 1 C beets

each serving provides:

calories	59	total fiber	4 g
total fat	0 g	protein	2 g
saturated fat	0 g	carbohydrates	12 g
cholesterol	0 mg	potassium	387 mg
sodium	88 mg		

deliciously healthy dinners

autumn salad

Prep time: 10 minutes
Cook time: 0 minutes

fruit and nuts make this salad a fun starter or side to most main-dish meals . . . and it can be served year round!

1	Granny Smith apple, rinsed and thinly sliced (with skin)
2 Tbsp	lemon juice
1 bag	mixed lettuce greens (or your favorite lettuce) (about 5 C), rinsed
½ C	dried cranberries
¼ C	walnuts, chopped
¼ C	unsalted sunflower seeds
⅓ C	low-fat raspberry vinaigrette dressing

1. Sprinkle lemon juice on the apple slices.
2. Mix the lettuce, cranberries, apple, walnuts, and sunflower seeds in a bowl.
3. Toss with raspberry vinaigrette dressing, to lightly cover the salad, and serve.

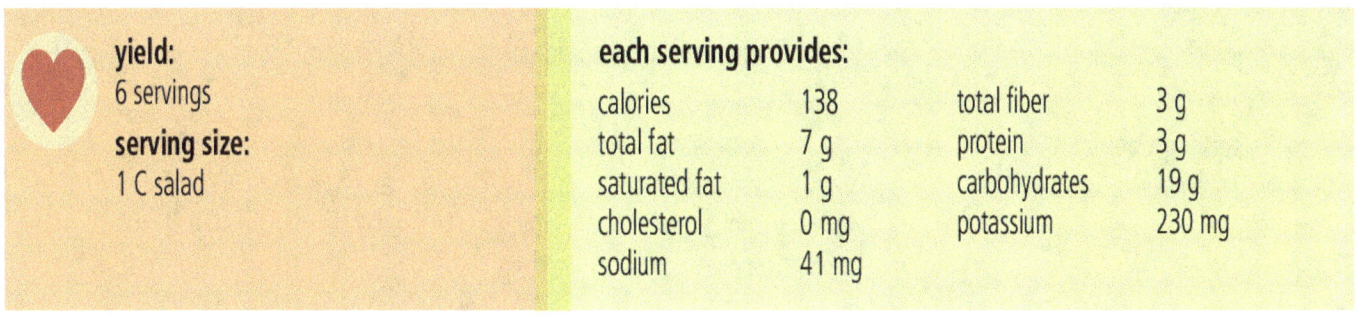

yield: 6 servings
serving size: 1 C salad

each serving provides:

calories	138	total fiber	3 g
total fat	7 g	protein	3 g
saturated fat	1 g	carbohydrates	19 g
cholesterol	0 mg	potassium	230 mg
sodium	41 mg		

limas and spinach

Prep time: 10 minutes
Cook time: 15 minutes

not your mother's lima beans, this dish is full of flavor as well as fiber

2 C	frozen lima beans
½ C	onion, chopped
1 C	fennel bulb, rinsed and cut into 4-inch strips
1 Tbsp	vegetable oil
¼ C	low-sodium chicken broth
1 bag	(10 oz) leaf spinach, rinsed
1 Tbsp	distilled vinegar
⅛ tsp	ground black pepper
1 Tbsp	dried chives

1. In a saucepan, steam or boil lima beans in unsalted water for about 10 minutes. Drain.
2. In sauté pan, sauté onion and fennel in oil.
3. Add beans and chicken broth to sauté pan, and cover. Cook for 2 minutes.
4. Stir in spinach. Cover and cook until spinach has wilted, about 2 minutes.
5. Stir in vinegar and pepper. Cover and let stand for 30 seconds.
6. Sprinkle with chives and serve.

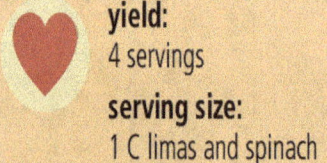

yield: 4 servings
serving size: 1 C limas and spinach

each serving provides:

calories	93	total fiber	6 g
total fat	2 g	protein	5 g
saturated fat	1 g	carbohydrates	15 g
cholesterol	0 mg	potassium	452 mg
sodium	84 mg		

deliciously healthy dinners

cinnamon-glazed baby carrots

Prep time: 3 minutes
Cook time: 11 minutes

no one will be able to resist this sweet veggie side dish that's great with most meat, chicken, and seafood

4 C	baby carrots, rinsed and split lengthwise if very thick (or frozen presliced carrots)
2 Tbsp	soft tub margarine
2 Tbsp	brown sugar
½ tsp	ground cinnamon
⅛ tsp	salt

1. Place the carrots in a small saucepan. Add just enough water to barely cover the carrots. Cover. Bring to a boil. Reduce heat to medium. Cook for 7–8 minutes, just until the carrots are easily pierced with a sharp knife.

2. While the carrots are cooking, combine margarine, brown sugar, cinnamon, and salt in a small saucepan, and melt together over low heat (or put in a microwave-safe bowl and microwave for a few seconds on high power, until margarine is mostly melted). Stir well to combine ingredients.

3. Drain carrots, leaving them in the saucepan. Pour cinnamon mixture over carrots. Cook and stir over medium heat for 2–3 minutes, just until the carrots are thoroughly coated and the glaze thickens slightly. Serve warm.

side dishes

vegetable

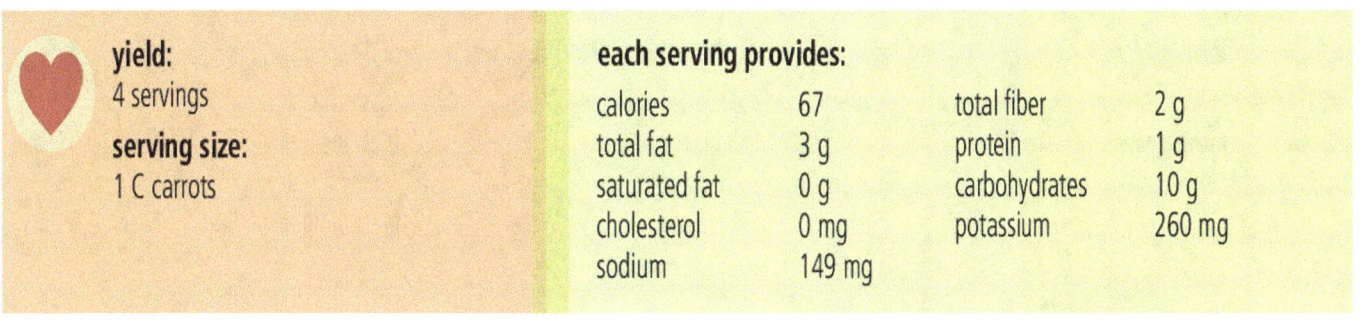

yield: 4 servings
serving size: 1 C carrots

each serving provides:

calories	67	total fiber	2 g
total fat	3 g	protein	1 g
saturated fat	0 g	carbohydrates	10 g
cholesterol	0 mg	potassium	260 mg
sodium	149 mg		

deliciously healthy dinners

creamy squash soup with shredded apples

Prep time: 10 minutes
Cook time: 20 minutes

this quick-to-fix soup is bursting with warm-you-up-flavor—serve with a crisp green salad and crusty whole-wheat bread

2 boxes	(16 oz each) of frozen pureed winter (butternut) squash
2	medium apples (try Golden Delicious or Gala)
1 Tbsp	olive oil
½ tsp	pumpkin pie spice
2 cans	(12 oz each) fat-free evaporated milk
¼ tsp	salt
⅛ tsp	ground black pepper

1. Place the frozen squash in a microwave-safe dish. Cover loosely. Defrost in the microwave on medium power for 5–10 minutes, until mostly thawed.

2. Meanwhile, peel then shred the apples using a grater or food processor, or peel and finely chop apples into thin strips. Set aside ¼ cup.

3. Warm oil in a 4-quart saucepan over medium heat. Add all but ¼ cup of the apples. Cook and stir until apples soften, about 5 minutes.

4. Stir in thawed squash and pumpkin pie spice.

5. Add the evaporated milk about ½ cup at a time, stirring after each addition.

6. Season with salt and pepper.

7. Cook and stir over high heat just until soup is about to boil.

8. Ladle into individual soup bowls. Top each with a tablespoon of the unused apples. Sprinkle with additional pumpkin pie spice if desired, and serve.

Tip: For chunkier soup, try two bags (14 oz each) frozen diced butternut squash. Or, cut a fresh butternut into small chunks, and place in a microwave-safe dish covered with 1 inch of water. Microwave on high for 5–10 minutes, or until squash is tender and can be easily pierced with a fork. Remove skin. Place squash in blender until desired consistency.

yield: 4 servings
serving size: 1½ C soup

each serving provides:

calories	334	total fiber	5 g
total fat	4 g	protein	18 g
saturated fat	1 g	carbohydrates	62 g
cholesterol	7 mg	potassium	1,142 mg
sodium	370 mg		

couscous with carrots, walnuts, and raisins

Prep time: 5 minutes
Cook time: 12 minutes

this quick-cooking grain dish has a touch of sweet and nutty flavors to go with most main dishes

1 C	couscous *(try whole-wheat couscous)*
1 tsp	olive oil
2 Tbsp	walnuts, coarsely chopped
¼ tsp	salt
⅛ tsp	black pepper
½ tsp	pumpkin pie spice or cinnamon
1⅓ C	water
2 Tbsp	raisins
½ C	carrots, rinsed, peeled, and shredded or thinly sliced; cut in half

1. In a 4-quart saucepan over medium heat, cook and stir couscous, olive oil, walnuts, salt, pepper, and spice just until couscous begins to brown.
2. Slowly add water, then raisins and carrots. Cover. Bring to a boil over high heat.
3. Remove from the heat, and let stand for 10 minutes.
4. Fluff with a fork. Serve immediately.

yield: 4 servings

serving size: ½ C couscous

each serving provides:

calories	218	total fiber	3 g
total fat	4 g	protein	6 g
saturated fat	0 g	carbohydrates	39 g
cholesterol	0 mg	potassium	168 mg
sodium	155 mg		

side dishes

grain

deliciously healthy dinners

quinoa with paprika and cumin

Prep time: 5 minutes
Cook time: 15 minutes

quinoa (pronounced KEEN-wah) is a grain native to South America and makes a great side dish for lean meats and seafood

1 C	quinoa
¼ tsp	salt
½ tsp	paprika (or try smoked paprika for a unique flavor)
½ tsp	ground cumin

1. Rinse quinoa in a fine mesh colander.
2. Place all ingredients in a saucepan with 2 cups of water. Cover.
3. Bring to a boil over high heat.
4. Reduce heat. Simmer for 10–15 minutes or until all water is absorbed.
5. Serve immediately, or refrigerate to reheat later.

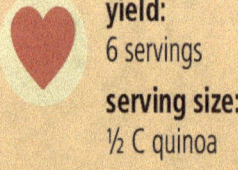

yield:
6 servings

serving size:
½ C quinoa

each serving provides:

calories	107	total fiber	2 g
total fat	2 g	protein	4 g
saturated fat	0 g	carbohydrates	20 g
cholesterol	0 mg	potassium	212 mg
sodium	103 mg		

good-for-you cornbread

Prep time: 10 minutes
Cook time: 25 minutes

try this healthier version of a classic comfort food with soups, salads, or the **Cornbread-Crusted Turkey** (on page 32) or **Three-Bean Chili With Chunky Tomatoes** (on page 92)

1 C	cornmeal
1 C	flour
¼ C	sugar
1 tsp	baking powder
1 C	low-fat (1 percent) buttermilk
1	large egg
¼ C	soft tub margarine
1 tsp	vegetable oil (to grease baking pan)

1. Preheat oven to 350 °F.
2. Mix together cornmeal, flour, sugar, and baking powder.
3. In another bowl, combine buttermilk and egg. Beat lightly.
4. Slowly add buttermilk and egg mixture to dry ingredients.
5. Add margarine and mix by hand or with mixer for 1 minute.
6. Bake for 20–25 minutes in an 8- by 8-inch, greased baking dish. Cool. Cut into 10 squares.

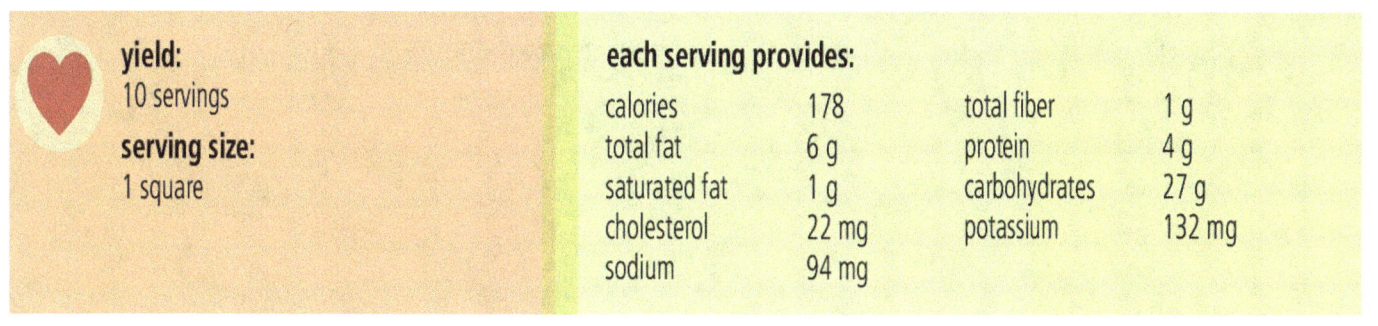

yield: 10 servings
serving size: 1 square

each serving provides:

calories	178	total fiber	1 g
total fat	6 g	protein	4 g
saturated fat	1 g	carbohydrates	27 g
cholesterol	22 mg	potassium	132 mg
sodium	94 mg		

side dishes
grain

savory brown rice

Prep time: 10 minutes
Cook time: 25 minutes

this savory, rich side dish is great with steak, pork, and chicken dishes

1 Tbsp	olive oil
1 C	onion, chopped
1 C	portabella mushrooms, rinsed, halved, then thinly sliced
½ C	celery, rinsed and finely diced
2 C	low-sodium chicken broth
1 C	instant brown rice, uncooked
¼ C	dried parsley
¼ tsp	salt
Ground black pepper to taste	

1. In a 4-quart saucepan, warm olive oil over medium heat. Add onion, mushrooms, and celery. Cook and stir for 5–7 minutes, until all vegetables are soft, but not brown.

2. Stir in the chicken broth, brown rice, parsley, salt, and pepper. Cover. Bring to a boil over high heat.

3. Reduce heat to medium. Cook according to brown rice package directions, about 5–10 minutes. Drain off any excess liquid. Fluff with a fork. Serve immediately.

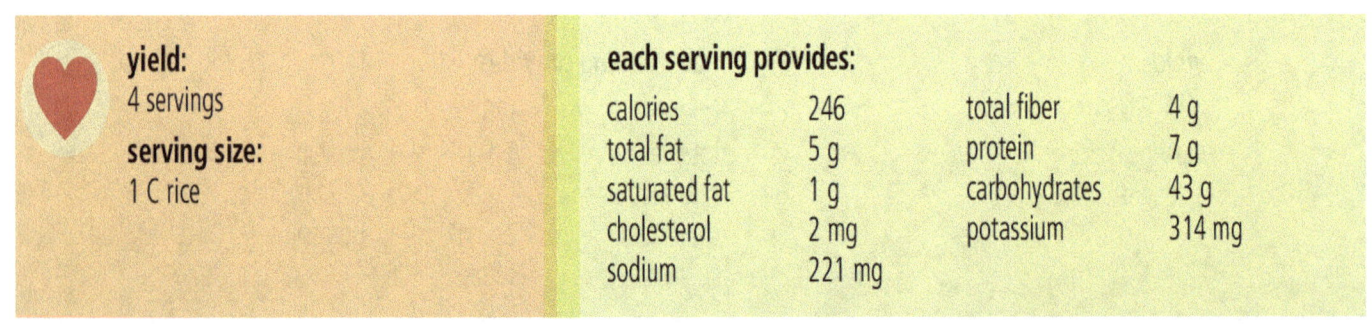

yield: 4 servings
serving size: 1 C rice

each serving provides:

calories	246	total fiber	4 g
total fat	5 g	protein	7 g
saturated fat	1 g	carbohydrates	43 g
cholesterol	2 mg	potassium	314 mg
sodium	221 mg		

kasha with bell pepper confetti

Prep time: 15 minutes
Cook time: 20 minutes

kasha, also known as buckwheat, is a nutty, fast-cooking whole grain that adds flavor to any meal

2 tsp	olive oil
½ C	onion, diced
¼ C	red bell pepper, rinsed and diced
¼ C	green bell pepper, rinsed and diced
¼ C	yellow bell pepper, rinsed and diced
1 can	(14½ oz) low-sodium chicken broth
¾ C	kasha
¼ tsp	dried oregano
½ tsp	salt
¼ tsp	ground black pepper

1. Heat oil in a 4-quart saucepan over medium heat. Add onion. Cook for 5 minutes, stirring occasionally.
2. Add bell peppers to saucepan. Cook and stir for 2 minutes. Remove vegetables from pan and set aside.
3. Add chicken broth to saucepan. Cover. Bring to a boil over high heat.
4. Stir in kasha. Reduce heat to medium-low. Cover. Simmer for about 10 minutes, until kasha is cooked and liquid is absorbed.
5. Stir in peppers and onion mixture, oregano, salt, and pepper. Heat for 1 minute. Serve immediately.

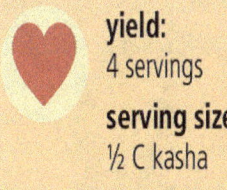

yield: 4 servings
serving size: ½ C kasha

each serving provides:

calories	144	total fiber	4 g
total fat	3 g	protein	4 g
saturated fat	0.5 g	carbohydrates	27 g
cholesterol	0 mg	potassium	180 mg
sodium	303 mg		

parmesan rice and pasta pilaf

Prep time: 10 minutes
Cook time: 25 minutes

this unique pasta and pilaf combination is a tasty side dish that goes well with most main dishes

2 Tbsp	olive oil
½ C	thin spaghetti (vermicelli), finely broken, uncooked
2 Tbsp	onion, diced
1 C	long-grain white rice, uncooked
1¼ C	chicken broth, hot
1¼ C	water, hot
¼ tsp	ground white pepper
1	bay leaf
2 Tbsp	shredded parmesan cheese

1. In a large sauté pan, heat the oil. Sauté vermicelli and onion until golden brown (for about 2–4 minutes) over medium-high heat. Drain off oil.

2. Add rice, chicken broth, water, pepper, and bay leaf. Cover and simmer for 15–20 minutes. Fluff with fork. Cover and let stand for 5 minutes. Remove bay leaf.

3. Sprinkle with shredded parmesan cheese, and serve immediately.

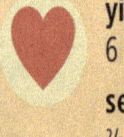

yield: 6 servings
serving size: ⅔ C pilaf

each serving provides:

calories	208	total fiber	1 g
total fat	6 g	protein	5 g
saturated fat	1 g	carbohydrates	33 g
cholesterol	2 mg	potassium	90 mg
sodium	140 mg		

deliciously healthy dinners

pesto baked polenta

Prep time: 10 minutes
Cook time: 10 minutes

instant whole-grain cornmeal (polenta), available in most grocery stores, provides a unique twist on a traditional Native American dish—and it's quick to fix

¼ tsp	salt
⅛ tsp	ground black pepper
1 C	fine yellow (instant) whole-grain cornmeal (polenta)
⅔ C	shredded parmesan cheese
¼ C	pesto sauce

1. Fill a 4-quart saucepan with 3 cups water; add salt and pepper. Cover. Bring to a boil over high heat.

2. When water boils, reduce heat to medium. Using a whisk or rubber spatula, quickly stir in cornmeal (polenta), cheese, and pesto sauce. Continue stirring until well blended and thick, about 1 minute.

3. Remove from heat. Pour the cornmeal mixture into an 8-inch pie pan or oven-safe dish. Spread evenly with the back of a spoon. Let stand until firm, about 5 minutes.

4. Preheat oven to 400 °F. Bake polenta until heated through, about 10 minutes. Remove from oven.

5. Cut into eight wedges. Serve hot.

side dishes — grain

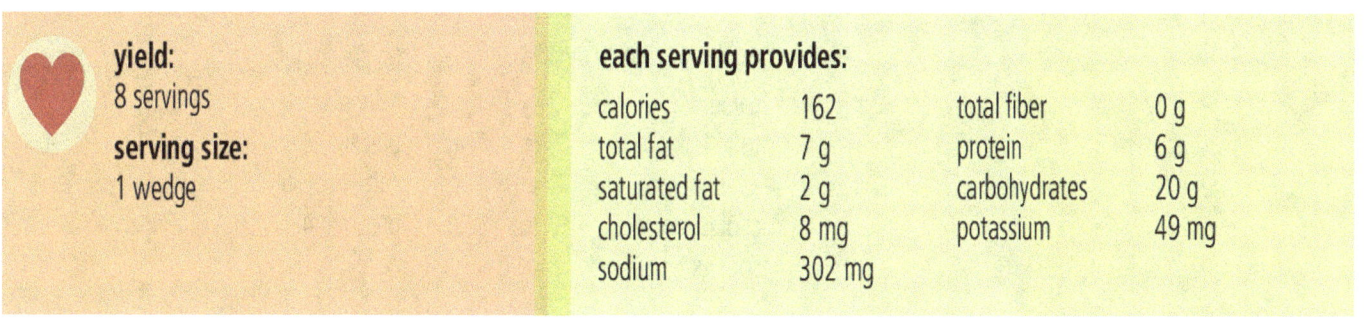

yield: 8 servings
serving size: 1 wedge

each serving provides:

calories	162	total fiber	0 g
total fat	7 g	protein	6 g
saturated fat	2 g	carbohydrates	20 g
cholesterol	8 mg	potassium	49 mg
sodium	302 mg		

sunshine rice

Prep time: 5 minutes
Cook time: 10 minutes

a citrus taste, combined with almonds, celery, and onions—but no added salt—makes this side dish a new classic . . . try it with fish!

- 1½ Tbsp vegetable oil
- 1¼ C celery, with leaves, rinsed and finely chopped
- 1½ C onion, finely chopped
- 1 C water
- ½ C orange juice
- 2 Tbsp lemon juice
- Dash hot sauce
- 1 C instant white rice, uncooked
- ¼ C slivered almonds

1. Heat oil in a medium-sized saucepan. Add celery and onion, and sauté until tender (about 10 minutes).
2. Add water, juices, and hot sauce. Bring to a boil over high heat.
3. Stir in rice, and bring back to a boil. Cover and turn heat down to simmer until rice is tender and liquid is absorbed, about 5–10 minutes.
4. Stir in almonds. Serve immediately.

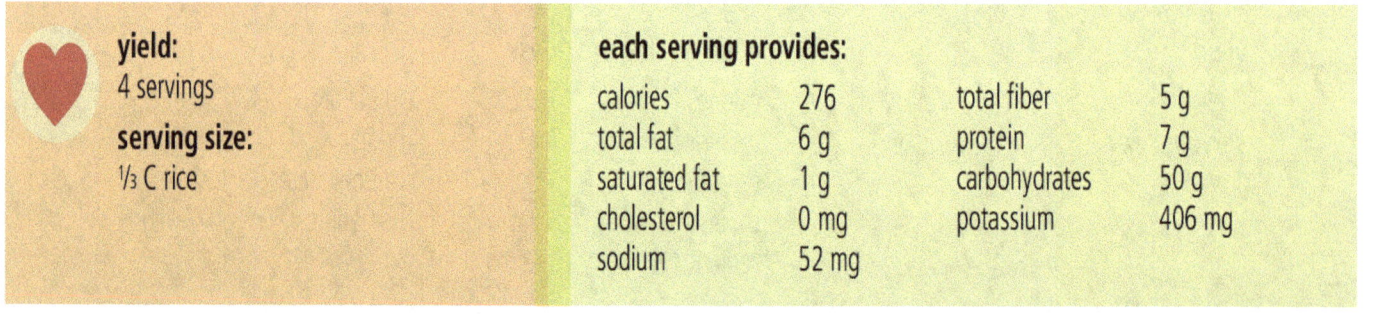

yield: 4 servings

serving size: ⅓ C rice

each serving provides:

calories	276	total fiber	5 g
total fat	6 g	protein	7 g
saturated fat	1 g	carbohydrates	50 g
cholesterol	0 mg	potassium	406 mg
sodium	52 mg		

www.ingramcontent.com/pod-product-compliance
Lightning Source LLC
Chambersburg PA
CBHW081624100526
44590CB00021B/3588